THE OLD ENGLISH
METRICAL PSALTER

GARLAND REFERENCE LIBRARY
OF THE HUMANITIES
(VOL. 189)

THE OLD ENGLISH METRICAL PSALTER
An Annotated Set of Collation Lists with the Psalter Glosses

Sarah Larratt Keefer

GARLAND PUBLISHING, INC. • NEW YORK & LONDON
1979

© 1979 Sarah Larratt Keefer
All rights reserved

Library of Congress Cataloging in Publication Data
Keefer, Sarah Larratt.
  The old English metrical psalter.
  (Garland reference library of the humanities ; v. 189)
  Bibliography: p.
  1. Anglo-Saxon poetry—Concordances. 2. Catholic
Church. Liturgy and ritual. [Psalter (Paris psalter)]—
Concordances. 3. Bible. O.T. Psalms. Anglo-Saxon—
Version. 4. Anglo-Saxon language—Glossaries,
vocabularies, etc. I. Title.
PR203.K37   829'.1   79-7920
ISBN 0-8240-9538-3

Printed on acid-free, 250-year-life paper
Manufactured in the United States of America

CONTENTS

Acknowledgements vii
Preface ix
Sigla List xi

Chapter I: The Tenth Century Reform 1

Chapter II: Materials and Approach 17

Chapter III: Tabulation and Results 47

Chapter IV: Conclusions and Postulations 143

Appendix: Typescript of Psalm-Texts 163

Bibliography 199

ACKNOWLEDGEMENTS

The author gratefully acknowledges the financial assistance of the Canada Council for her doctoral research; the generous access to the Dictionary of Old English Library (Toronto); the unfailing advice and support of her advisor, Angus F. Cameron; the encouragement and suggestions provided by her husband, her father and her mother; and the cheerful dedication of her typist, Else Irvine. To all the others who helped me with the project, but who are unnamed here, I also extend my heartfelt thanks.

Sarah Larratt Keefer
July, 1979
Peterborough, Ontario

PREFACE

In my study of Old English poetry, I have found that I am increasingly disturbed by vague terms such as 'Cædmonian' or 'Cynewulfian' school of writing, and by the assumption that these 'schools' were made up of creative members of secular pre-Conquest English society. I prefer to regard much of the extant Old English verse as a product of the ecclesiastical system in its various forms, a system which may have brought a singular influence to bear upon vernacular verse-making. It is my belief that such an influence can, in fact, be established, and that it is one which will shed light on the origins and purposes behind much of the Old English metrical canon. The singular influence to which I refer is that of the Christian liturgy, which in places is found to be explicit in phraseology or intention, and in places implicit in theme or allusion.

In order to establish an ecclesiastical background and a liturgical influence for Old English poetry, we must both examine the nature of the poems preserved, and sort out their generic and thematic content. An analysis of the entire canon is impossible here, so a distinction must be made forthwith, between the genres of poetic composition and poetic paraphrase. I view poetic composition as that verse whose source is either original or based on traditional folklore and legend, while poetic paraphrase would seem to suggest that verse which deliberately sets out to develop into meter an established, specific and certainly written source. In the latter category we can place the *Genesis*, *Exodus*, *Daniel* and *Azarias* of the so-called 'Cædmonian school', the *Meters of Boethius*, the Benedictine Office preces and prayers from MSS Bodleian Junius 121 and Corpus Christi College, Cambridge 201, the Kentish *Psalm 50*, and the *Paris Psalter poetry*. To the former, we would naturally assign *Beowulf* and other heroic verse, *Christ and Satan*, the rest of the *Exeter* and *Vercelli* miscellaneous pieces, the metrical Saints' Lives, and the remaining minor poems.

Because liturgy is an established written source, it would appear to have more in common with the genre of poetic paraphrase than with that of poetic composition. I shall, therefore, for the purposes of this thesis, confine myself to the study of poetic paraphrase. After giving a brief historical background of monasticism as my introduction, I shall describe my chosen liturgical and metrical materials, and shall present, as the core of my thesis, a methodology of correlation, with application and tabulated results, by which Old English poetic paraphrase and the influence of the liturgy upon it may be examined.

It would seem logical, in a study of this kind, to begin with those examples of metrical verse which display the most apparent relationship to the liturgy. Accordingly, I shall here consider the Book of Psalms as one of the principal examples of liturgical influence on Old English poetry. My reasons for this choice are many: the Psalms pervade all aspects of the liturgy; they are the fundamental element of the Benedictine Daily Offices; they were the first Biblical or liturgical selections used by monks and scholars alike in their study of Latin; and we possess a large number of Latin Psalters from pre-Conquest England which carry almost-complete Old English interlinear glosses. Finally, there remain the fragments of a remarkable paraphrase of the Book of Psalms, which are extant in the Old English metrical canon. In the following chapters, I shall, therefore, concern myself with a study of this metrical psalter as an example of Old English poetic paraphrase which was influenced by the liturgy.

As I hope to show in the following pages, this complete vernacular metrical paraphrase of the Psalter was produced in the same century that saw the high watermark of Benedictine education in Anglo-Saxon England. It is my intention to examine the remains of this paraphrase in some detail, proposing liturgical traditions behind it and, accordingly, suggesting the era, location and perhaps the social climate which produced it.

THE OLD ENGLISH INTERLINEAR GLOSSED PSALTER SIGLA

AFTER A.S. Cook, *Biblical Quotations in Old English Prose Writers* (London: 1898), and U. Lindelöf, *Studien zu altenglischen Psalterglossen* (*Bonner Beiträge zur Anglistik* XIII, Bonn: 1914).

A. BL MS Cotton Vespasian A.i: *The Vespasian Psalter.*
B. Bodleian MS Junius 27: *The Junius Psalter.*
C. Cambridge University Library MS Ff.i.23: *The Cambridge Psalter.*
D. BL MS Royal 2.B.v: *The Regius Psalter.*
E. Trinity College, Cambridge MS R 17.i: *Eadwine's Canterbury Psalter.*
F. BL MS Stowe 2: *The Spelman* or *Stowe Psalter.*
G. BL MS Cotton Vitellius E. xviii: *The Vitellius Psalter.*
H. BL MS Cotton Tiberius C.vi: *The Tiberius Psalter.*
I. Lambeth Palace (London) MS 427: *The Lambeth Psalter.*
J. BL MS Arundel 60: *The Arundel Psalter.*
K. Salisbury Cathedral MS 150: *The Salisbury Psalter.*
L. BL Additional MS 37517: *The Bosworth Psalter.*
M. Morgan Library. New York MS M 776: *The Lothian* or *Blickling Psalter.*

and added to these interlinear glossed psalters is the partly metrical, partly prose vernacular parallel translation of the Psalter:

P. Paris Bibliothèque Nationale MS Fonds Latin 8824: *The Paris Psalter.*

To this list I would add my own provisional siglum V, for the original for the metrical part of P. Hence:

V. Paris Bibliothèque Nationale MS Fonds Latin 8824, fols. 64a–175b (Vp); Bodleian MS Junius 121, fols. 42a–53b (Vj); BL MS Cotton Tiberius B.i. in the poem *Menologium*, 11. 60–62 (Vm); and Trinity College, Cambridge MS R 17.i, pss. 90: 15–95: 2 (Ve): *The Old English Metrical Psalter*.

CHAPTER I: THE TENTH CENTURY REFORM

The Book of Psalms from the Old Testament was held in high esteem both as messianic scripture and as devotional prayers by the Church Fathers. St. Jerome issued three separate translations of the Psalter[1]: a version, thought to be the 'Roman' or 'Romanum', based entirely on the Septuagint and produced ca 384; a version, called 'Gallican' or 'Gallicanum', which was based on Origen's Hexaplaric text of the Septuagint, and issued ca 392, and the Hebrew Psalter, which Jerome translated directly from the Hebrew text ca 400. Of the three, only the first two versions will concern this study.[2]

When St. Benedict of Nursia (ca 480-550) founded his Order and established his Rule, he incorporated the Psalter into the Rule, to be said regularly by the Order in canonical Hours. These Hours are called the Opus Dei, or Divine Office, and consist of eight periods[3], three hours apart throughout the day, at which certain psalms, prayers, and lessons are read. These selections are so arranged that the complete Psalter is said every week. The Opus Dei regulated the life of the Benedictine monasteries, and focussed Benedictinism on prayer and contemplation. Later on, St. Benedict of Aniane (ca 750-821) began the French monastic reform by recodifying and systematizing the original Rule. His revised document, known as the Codex Regularum[4], was approved by the Synod of Aachen in 817, and was later adopted for use in the English Church by the Tenth Century Reformers. Hence, the Psalter, although technically termed 'aliturgical synaxis' (to be distinguished from liturgical synaxis which describes the celebration of the Eucharist) may be seen as functional in a liturgical sense in the Opus Dei. It is with this simplified definition in mind that we refer to the psalters of this study as 'liturgy' and 'liturgical', rather than as 'synaxis' or 'synactic'.

When St. Augustine came to Canterbury in 597, he brought with him the Romanum textual version of the Psalter. Monasticism took root in England early, both through Augustine's Kentish settlement, and through a mission sent to Northumbria by the Irish monk Columba of Iona (ca 563). The great house of Lindisfarne was set up on the north-east coast of England by Columba's successor Aidan, establishing a major monastery and bishopric under the ægis of the Irish Church. Later, the Irish monks withdrew from Northumbria following the Synod of Whitby in 663, and the Irish foundation in Northumbria fell under English Benedictine jurisdiction.

Benedictine schools were set up in the seventh and eighth centuries, and learning flourished under scholars such as Aldhelm, Bede and Alcuin. Then, the Danish raids, beginning between 786 and 802, put an end to this period of Benedictine intellectual creativity and, by the end of the ninth century, the Northumbrian seats of learning had all been sacked and abandoned, and the southern houses at about the same time had fallen into decay of every sort. It was the tenth century which saw the rebuilding of the Benedictine monastic system in England, and it is this period of the Tenth Century Reform which is relevant to this dissertation.

The Danish invasions of the ninth century shattered the English Church as its members had known it. Indeed, society itself declined, and a desire for education fell away from a people intent on merely remaining alive and independent of external and foreign dominance. Yet while the Danish raids themselves did the Church much damage, the consequences of the raids did more. That men were constantly levied into makeshift armies meant that fields were abandoned, trades forgotten or poorly followed, and that no one had leisure to consider leaving the duties of secular society to become a monk. This state of affairs concerned King Alfred, as we can see from his celebrated Preface to the Cura Pastoralis:

> Swæ clæne hio wæs oðfeallenu on
> Angelcynne ðæt swiðe feawa wæron
> behionan Humbre ðe hiora ðeninga
> cuðen understondan on Englisc oððe
> furðum an ærendgewrit of Lædene
> on Englisc areccean; ond ic wene
> ðætte noht monige begiondan Humbre
> næren.[5]

In the same Preface, he sets out his plans for educating his people, and for rejuvenating the monastic order: "Lære mon siððan furður on Lædengeðiode ða ðe mon furðor læran wille and to hierran hade don wille."[6] Yet, while Asser tells us[7] that Alfred founded two monasteries, one for men and another for women, he was in fact obliged to people his houses with monks and nuns from the Continent. His settlement was made at Athelney, yet it failed to flourish as Alfred had hoped. Little mention is made of it before the Tenth Century Reform. Alfred's son Edward established a further foundation at New Minster, Winchester, which, however, was ruled by a foreign abbot, Grimbald of St. Bertin. This foundation does not

4

appear to have been fully monastic[8], and eventually collapsed, together with the rest of Alfred's attempts at monastic revival, long before the Reform.

The kings between Alfred and Edgar had little time or inclination for the restoring of monasticism and education at home. Alfred's son Edward spent most of his life re-establishing the military power of Wessex so that, by 924, every Danish colony south of the Humber had been absorbed. His son, Athelstan, who is celebrated with his brother Edmund in the Chronicle poem The Battle of Brunanburh, furthered the supremacy of Wessex to include virtually all of England. He then turned his attention to the affairs of the Continent. While he is said to have collected relics and maintained contacts with foreign monasteries[9], his wide-sweeping military involvements left him no time to re-organize the shattered monastic houses of England.

Athelstan's brother Edmund succeeded him in 939, but spent his whole reign involved in domestic struggles with the Danes of the Humber region in England, and in the politics of the Franks on the Continent. Their brother Eadred, when he succeeded, was more concerned with England, and although he was the first king in the tenth century to show an interest in monastic reform at home, he again had little time in which to pursue such undertakings. His reign was chiefly spent in conflict with the Danes in Northumbria, and in recovering West Saxon supremacy throughout England.

Eadwig, son of Edmund, came to the throne in 955, a year which marks the first period since the reign of Alfred in which England was actually free from the threat of invasion. But Eadwig was unsympathetic to the incipient Reform, and banished Dunstan, its leader, to the Continent. A local revolt in England placed Eadwig's brother Edgar in command of Mercia; he promptly recalled Dunstan and, on Eadwig's death and Edgar's succession in 959, gave him the sees of Worcester and London, later transferring him to Canterbury in 960.

It is King Edgar who stands out in history as the royal patron of the Benedictine Reform of the tenth century. His enthusiastic support and participation enabled the three great Reformers (Dunstan, Æthelwold and Oswald) to carry out educational and canonical revivals and refoundations. During this period of peace which he so carefully preserved, the age of Old English Benedictine homiletic writing came into its own.

The great achievement of the tenth century was the restoration of the powers of the English Church, and the efflorescence of learning, accomplished largely through the efforts of archbishop Dunstan, and his friends and disciples, Æthelwold and Oswald; in short, the tenth century reform movement.[10]

The work of reform, the obvious next step after the revival of military and economic strength in Wessex, was brought about by the combined efforts of the three Benedictine monks, Dunstan, Æthelwold and Oswald. Dunstan[11], the leader of the Reform movement, was born ca 910, of a noble family from near Glastonbury where he studied as a boy. His life career was intended to be the West Saxon court, but he chose rather the simple celibacy of a monk, and made his profession to Ælfheah, Bishop of Winchester, who later ordained him.

Dunstan's decision had made him unpopular with Edmund (who had ascended the throne in 939), but he eventually accepted Dunstan's choice, and later installed him as Abbot of Glastonbury. Dunstan held Glastonbury for the period 940-955, during which time he organized the first proper Benedictine community of monks in England since the time of the Danish raids. Eadred, who became king in 946, was sympathetic to Dunstan's endeavors, and so the Glastonbury community flourished during this period.

During the brief reign of Eadwig, Dunstan was exiled to the Continent after a personal confrontation with the king. When Edgar replaced Eadwig as king of Mercia, he recalled Dunstan, as we have already seen. When Edgar gave Dunstan the see of Canterbury in 960, he replaced him at Worcester with one of the other two Reformers, Dunstan's pupil Oswald.[12] In 964, Edgar granted Winchester to Dunstan's other pupil, Æthelwold, the third Reformer.[13] Earlier, Eadred had given Æthelwold the abandoned foundation of Abingdon, which he had peopled with Glastonbury monks.[14] Thus, the wealthiest sees in England were placed in the hands of those three men whom Edgar knew would effectively carry through his desire to re-establish English Benedictinism.

Dunstan's main work was foundation and re-foundation, with Glastonbury as his greatest accomplishment. After 959, he re-established houses at Malmesbury, Bath, and Westminster. The Glastonbury monks also helped to found Benedictine houses at Milton and Exeter, and to establish daughter houses to Glastonbury at Muchelney, and at Alfred's defunct settlement at Athelney. Before his death, Dunstan also saw four other houses come into existence, all connected with Glastonbury; these were Cerne Abbas, Tavistock, Horton and Cranborne.

As bishop, Oswald transformed the clerks at Worcester into a proper monastic community, monasticised the neighboring sees of Crediton and Wells, later re-established the abbey at Winchcombe, and placed monks again at Ripon. He brought fellow monks, Germanus and the great educator Abbo, from Fleury where he had studied, to rule and teach at his newly-founded Anglian abbey of Ramsey, and these men began to restore the level of learning lost in the period of the Danish invasions.

Æthelwold has been considered by historians to be both the greatest and the most authoritarian of these three. He drove the sedentary clerks out of his see of Winchester in 964, replacing them with Abingdon and Glastonbury monks, and he also set about restoring monasticism in the area of the Danelaw to the east. He refounded Medeshamstede (Peterborough) in 966, Ely in 970, and Thorney in 972, and expanded both Barrow-on-Humber and Breedon in Leicester into monastic houses. Croyland, St. Neot's at Chertsey, and St. Alban's have also been attributed to Æthelwold's work.

Yet while these activities mark the outward manifestation of the Reform, there is evidence of some internal conflict[15] between the policies of the Reformers. Dunstan maintained a rule which was the most fully English of the three; Æthelwold's tradition contained some Continental elements, and Oswald's was strongly influenced by Fleury, where he had been sent to study in 950. Edgar realized the pressing need for unity among the Reformers, and that the movement might otherwise destroy itself through faction, so he insisted[16] upon the holding of a council at which a common way of life would be decided, which would be put under the royal patronage of the king and queen.[17]

It is perhaps important here to recognize Edgar's ability and energy in his role as organizer of the Reform. In the words of the Hyde annalist: "Eadgarus vir strenuissimus nemini priorum in temporali gloria vel divinitatis amore secundus."[18] The Proem to the Regularis Concordia[19] gives him full credit for the initiation of the Winchester Synod which was held some time between 965 and 975.[20] At this council, which was modeled on the Synod of Aachen of 817, the great document of unity, called Regularis Concordia Anglicae nationis monachorum sanctimonialiumque was prepared. It made provision for continental influence which was represented at the Synod by monks from Fleury and Ghent, and drew on continental Benedictine documents, especially the Ordo qualiter, the Rule for Canons, and the Aachen capitula.[21] The final product was a codification of the Benedictine Rule which standardized its practice throughout England to the satisfaction of everyone, and which successfully united the practical objective of the Reform movement. Its Prologue, or Proem, is a long preface which gives the background and many of the events of the meeting in Winchester; thereafter the Concordia itself consists of chapters providing for liturgical functions of the day and year, and for monastic duties. It closes with specific prescriptions for ceremonies to be performed at the death of a monk, but significantly also outlines that the monasteries are to be free from the heriot, or death-tax, due to the king, and that the monks are obliged to pray for the king and queen as royal patrons.

> The basis therefore of the monastic life of the English revival was the normal use of western Europe, inherited in part, perhaps, from the traditions of Glastonbury and other English churches, but chiefly through information of training received from Fleury and Ghent. In other words, the life, now fully set on a level with contemporary monasticism abroad, was primarily liturgical and claustral, and contained the accretions of psalmody and vocal prayer, together with the elaborate execution of the chant, that had become normal in Europe.[22]

Since definite provisions for the Opus Dei were made in the Concordia, we may set the Psalter into the tenth century as an important liturgical element for the Benedictine Reform. Hence we may tentatively describe the Old English metrical Psalter as a vernacular translation of a vital aspect of Benedictinism, even as a Benedictine 'document'. Should we accept this label for the sake of the argument in hand, the complete vernacular metrical Psalter with which this dissertation concerns itself, and which may very possibly stem from the period of the Tenth Century Reform, occupies an interesting position in Anglo-Saxon literary history. As a vernacular translation of a Reform 'document', it stands in company with Æthelwold's translation of the Regula Sancti Benedicti, and with the later translations of the Regularis Concordia, but it is unusual in that it is in meter rather than in prose. It is also not unlike the interlinear glossed psalters[23] which were used for liturgical and educational purposes by the Benedictine order. However, it is again singular in that it is a poetic paraphrase, rather than a literal prose translation.

Æthelwold translated the Regula Sancti Benedicti, probably around 970[24] on the request of King Edgar, who rewarded him with the gift of the manor of Southburne for performing the task; this manor was subsequently given to the see of Ely.[25] Of the copies that were made of this vernacular translation, we have four manuscripts. The earliest (O)[26] is from the mid-tenth century: Oxford Corpus Christi College 197, fols. 1-105, which contains the Regula in Latin and English, together with some documents related to Bury St. Edmund, which were added at Bury in the eleventh century.[27] Corpus Christi College, Cambridge 178 (A), fols. 287-457, dates from the early eleventh century, and shows the Worcester 'tremulous hand'; BL Cotton Titus A.iv (T)[29], fols. 2-107, is from ca 1050; and BL Cotton Faustina A.x (F), fols. 102-148[30], which has an historical tractate appended to it[31], dates from the late eleventh century. Both Tupper[32] and Bateson[33] assign this tractate to Æthelwold from roughly the same era as the Regula translation.

Other manuscripts which contain vernacular translations of the Regula whose authorship is unknown, have been preserved as well. These are Durham Cathedral B.iv.24[34], BL Cotton Tiberius A.iii, fols. 118-163v[35], and a fragment from Wells Cathedral[36], from the mid-eleventh century; Corpus Christi College, Cambridge 57, which has an Anglo-Saxon gloss from early eleventh-century Abingdon[37]; and Trinity College, Cambridge O.2.30, which has a Latin version of the Regula in a tenth-century Irish hand, and Anglo-Saxon glosses at fols. 130v, 131r and 133v.[38] Cotton Tiberius A.iii, which contains an interlinear gloss to the Rule on fols. 118-163, also preserves a vernacular translation of Chapter IV of the Regula on fol. 103, and this fragment is also found in Gloucester Cathedral MS 35 as well. Finally, we have BL Cotton Claudius D.iii (C), a bilingual Regula from ca 1225 in early Middle English, used by the nuns at Wintney in Hampshire.[39] A complete study of the textual relationships outlined above, and of the manuscripts which I have listed, may be found in Mechthild Gretsch's article, "Æthelwold's Translation of the Regula Sancti Benedicti and its Latin Exemplar." [40]

We can therefore see that the remaining copies of Æthelwold's translation found their way to Worcester, and east to Bury St. Edmund perhaps by 1050. This suggests a fairly advanced dissemination process and, if the original of the copies was written by Æthelwold at Winchester in the mid-tenth century[41], we should regard Winchester as a highly productive distribution center at that time.

Historians are now divided about the identity of the author of the original Latin of the Regularis Concordia. On the supposedly-indefinite authority of Ælfric[42], scholars have assumed that Æthelwold was the author of the Concordia[43]. However, Symons states that the Concordia is an anonymous document, and that a century after it was written, it was regarded as Dunstan's work.[44] It was also translated into Old English, and exists today in two manuscripts: the fragments on fols. 3-27v and 174r-176v of BL Cotton Tiberius A.iii(L)[45], and fols. 1-7 of Corpus Christi College, Cambridge 201 (C). These fragments preserve selections of lines from the Concordia: ll. 170-257 in L, and ll. 612-753 in C.

Scholars are divided on the identity of the translator(s) of these fragments.[48] Older critics thought that L was the original document of the Eynsham letter, rather than a translation, Schröer refutes a connection between L and Ælfric, while Breck assumes one, describing L as being "in the Ælfrician dialect and manner." [49] Zupitza concludes that C and L are not merely fragmentary translations, but rather pieces of a postulated complete translation of the Concordia, and hence probably the work of one man who did not use the Concordia gloss for his project. However, since Zupitza rules out any connection between Ælfric and the L-fragment, he therefore excludes the possibility of Ælfric as this original translator. Tupper in part supports Zupitza in suggesting that L and C cannot safely be connected with Ælfric at all, and that therefore the Eynsham letter cannot be cited as authority for Æthelwold as the original

translator of the Concordia. Yet he prefers to view
Æthelwold as the author of the Latin Concordia, regardless
of who the translator(s) of L and C may have been.

The third vernacular gloss of a Benedictine document
appears on fols. 164-168 of BL Cotton Tiberius A.iii which,
to recapitulate, also contains vernacular glosses to the
Regula, the Concordia, a Concordia fragment, and a vernacular
translation of Chapter IV of the Regula. This document is
the Epitome of St. Benedict of Aniane,[50] identified by
Bateson as the latter part of the Memoriale qualiter in
monasterio conversare debemus,[51] and is an interlinear
vernacular gloss from the mid-eleventh century.

As we have said, the Psalter is a major part of the
Rule of Benedictinism, as shown by its practical application
in the Opus Dei. The Romanum text, which came to England
with St. Augustine, was prevalent until the time of the
Reform; thereafter, as part of the standardization of monastic
customs, the Gallicanum was introduced and, by the twelfth
century, it had virtually replaced the old Romanum in
Benedictine usage. There remain thirteen psalters from pre-
Conquest England which preserve Old English interlinear
glosses. We assume, from a study of these books, that they
were used to provide a vernacular translation to the liturgical Latin, and to teach scholars the Latin psalter-text.
We have of course no way of knowing the actual number of
interlinear glossed psalters which were written but, of the
thirteen left to us, nearly three-quarters were produced as
a result of the Tenth Century Reform. As we shall see, the
vernacular metrical psalter has also been assigned to the
tenth century. It is therefore against this historical
background, rich with vernacular translations of Benedictine-
related material, that we must set our analysis of the Old
English metrical Psalter. As a poetic paraphrase it is very
unusual amongst the vernacular prose translations of the era.
It is not, however, unprecedented, because the tenth century
can be seen to have been an age which accepted continental
and Latin material, and then naturally modified it with
English language and custom, in the process of adopting such
material as its own.

NOTES

1. F. N. Cross, ed. *The Oxford Dictionary of the Christian Church* (Oxford: 1958), p.1121.

2. A twelfth century psalter designated E and called *Eadwine's Canterbury Psalter* preserves Latin text from all three versions.

3. Called Mattins, Lauds, Prime, Terce, Sext, None, Vespers and Compline.

4. A. S. Napier has edited a vernacular version of the last part of the *Codex*, called the *Epitome*, in vol. 150, original series, of the Early English Text Society, together with other Benedictine reform documents.

5. D. Whitelock, ed., *Sweet's Anglo-Saxon Reader* (Oxford: 1967), p.5.

6. *Ibid.*, p.7.

7. Asser, *De Rebus Gestis Alfredi*, section 78, cited by Dom David Knowles in *The Monastic Order in England* (Cambridge: 1966), p.33.

8. cf. Knowles, p.33, note 1, for a discussion of the monastic life at St. Bertin. Notice especially the reference to William of Malmesbury, which suggests that Grimbald's tradition was one of canons, i.e., secular clerks.

9. J. Armitage Robinson, *The Times of St. Dunstan* (Oxford: 1923), pp.51-80.

10. Margaret Deanesly, *The PreConquest Church in England* (London: 1961), p.276.

11. The best authorities for Dunstan are the *Vita auctore B* from ca 1000, and the *Vita auctore Adelardo*, in W. Stubbs, ed., *Memorials of St. Dunstan* (Rolls Series 63. London: 1874).

12. The best authority for Oswald is the *Vita sancti Oswaldi auctore anonymo* in J. Raine, ed., *Historians of the Church of York* (Rolls Series 71. London: 1879-94), vol. I.

13. The best authority for Æthelwold is Ælfric's *Vita sancti Ethelwoldi* in Michael Winterbottom, ed., *Three Lives of English Saints*, (Toronto: 1972).

14. Winterbottom, ed., I: 7, on pp.19-20.

15. cf. Knowles, p.42.

16. for Edgar's participation, cf. *Proem* to the *Regularis Concordia* in Dom Thomas Symons, ed., *The Monastic Agreement of the Monks and Nuns of the English Nation* (London: 1953), pp.1-3.

17. cf. *Vita sancti Oswaldi auctore anonymo* in *Raine*, p.425.

18. *Liber Vitae*, p.7 in W. de G. Birch, ed., *The Liber Vitae of Hyde Abbey, Winchester* (Hampshire Record Society: 1892).

19. printed in the vernacular by O. Cockayne, ed., *Leechdoms, Wortcunning and Starcraft of Early England* (Rolls Series 35, London: 1864-1866), vol. III, pp.432-444, and in Latin by Symons, ed., *The Monastic Agreement between the Monks and Nuns of the English Nation*.

20. Knowles places it ca 972 in *The Monastic Order in England*, p.42, but for Symons' dating, see p.41 of Dom Thomas Symons, "Regularis Concordia: History and Derivation" in David Parsons, ed., *Tenth Century Studies: Essays in Commemoration of the Council of Winchester and the Regularis Concordia* (Chichester: 1975), pp.37-60.

21. for a more complete study, cf. Dom Thomas Symons, "Sources of the Regularis Concorida" in the *Downside Review* of 1941. pp.37-60.

22. Knowles, p.44.

23. to be fully described in Chapter II.

24. cf. F. Tupper's excellent article, "History and Texts of the Benedictine Reform of the Tenth Century", *Modern Language Review* 8 (1893), pp.344-367.

25. so noted in the Liber Eliensis, and referred to M. Bateson, "Rules for Monks and Secular Canons after the Revival under King Edgar", English Historical Review 9 (1894), p.692. Cf. also Mechthild Gretsch, Die Regula Sancti Benedicti in England und ihre altenglische Übersetzung (Munich: 1973), pp.9-11.

26. cf. F. Tupper article in M.L.R. for sigla assignment.

27. N. R. Ker, A Catalogue of Manuscripts Containing Anglo-Saxon (Oxford: 1953), p.430, item 353. Ed. A. Schröer, Die angelsächsischen Prosarbeitungen der Benediktinnerregel. Bibl. der ags. Prosa 2 (Kassel: 1885-1888). Repr. H. Gneuss, ed., Darmstadt: 1964.

28. Ker, p.60; item 41B. Ed., Schröer.

29. Ker, p.262; item 200, Ed., Schröer.

30. Ker, p.194; item 154B. Ed., Schröer.

31. Ed. O. Cockayne, Leechdoms, Wortcunning and Starcraft of Early England, III, pp.432-444.

32 Tupper, p.350.

33. Bateson, p.694.

34. Ker, p.148; item 109. Coll. G. Caro, "Die Varianten der Durhamer Hs. und des Tiberius-fragments der ae. Prosaversion der Benedictinnerregel", Englische Studien 24 (1898), pp.161-176.

35. Ker, p.240; item 186. Coll. Caro, and also ed. W. S. Logeman in E.E.T.S. 90.

36. Ker, p.464; item 395. Ed., Schröer.

37. Ker, p.46; item 34. Cf. Bateson for listing, and Gretsch, Die Regula Sancti Benedicti etc., p.126, for discussion.

38. Ker, p.137; item 94. Cf. Bateson and Gretsch as above.

39. Ker, p.xix, note 2. Ed.Schröer, Die Wintney-Version der Regula Sancti Benedicti (Halle: 1888).

40. Mechthild Gretsch, "Æthelwold's Translation of the Regula Sancti Benedicti and its Latin Exemplar", Anglo-Saxon England 3 (1974), pp.125-151.

41. As Helmut Gneuss would suggest in his discussion of the vernacular Regula in "The Origin of Standard Old English and Æthelwold"s School at Winchester", Anglo-Saxon England 1 (1972), pp.63-83.

42. In his Letter to the Monks of Eynsham, ed. M. Bateson (in Kitchin, ed., Obedientary Rolls of St. Swithun's, Hampshire Record Society: 1892) p.175, we read "Liber consuetudine quem sanctus athelwoldus uuintoniensis episcopus cum coepiscopis et abbatibus . . . . undique collegit ac monachis instituit observandum."

43. cf. Bateson, "Rules for Monks and Secular Canons", p.700, and Tupper, p.356.

44. Symons, pp.li-lii.

45. cf. Tupper article for sigla assignment.

46. Ed. A. Schröer, "De Consuetudine Monachorum", Englische Studien 9 (1886), pp.294-296, and E. Breck, Translation of Athelwold's De consuetudine monachorum (Leipzig: 1887).

47. Ed. J. Zupitza, "Ein weiteres Bruchstück der Regularis Concordia in altenglische Sprache", Archiv 84, (1890), pp.2-16.

48. Tupper summarizes these arguments in his article, pp. 358-363.

49. Breck, p.9.

50. Ed. A. S. Napier, in E.E.T.S., o.s. 150 (1916).

51. Bateson, "Rules for Monks and Secular Canons", p.699.

Chapter II: Materials and Approach

The Latin psalters which remain from Anglo-Saxon England are of both the Romanum and Gallicanum type. To their texts have been added interlinear translations in Old English, and marginal comments in both Latin and the vernacular. In some psalters, the gloss is continuous, indicating the intention by the glossator of providing as complete an Old English translation of the original as he could manage. In other psalters, we find evidence of educational, rather than liturgical glossing, since Latin lemmata are left unglossed if they are proper names or common vocabulary with which the glossator might already be familiar. It is, however, necessary to point out that the vernacular gloss of these psalters was not simply in each case the product of original translation from the text. It is because of the manner of providing glosses that we can trace the "traditions" of liturgical psalter-gloss, since the practice seems often to have been to copy the gloss from one book into another. We see, as evidence for this, that many of the Gallicana carry vernacular glosses which accord, not with the Latin in them, but with the older Romanum texts of other psalters. The glossators appear to have copied their translations directly from Romana into the newer Gallicana, and it was only their familiarity with Latin which determined the extent to which they altered the gloss to fit the new text to which it was being applied.

There had, of course, to be original translations, and these became the models for the copies, and hence the progenitors of the psalter-gloss traditions. Since the extant number of interlinear glossed psalters is so limited, and since we must assume[1] that there were many of these books made, our knowledge of gloss traditions must therefore be limited too. There are two distinct "families" of psalter-glosses traceable through most of the remaining codices: the Vespasian group, deriving from the Vespasian Psalter[2], and the Regius group, deriving from the Regius Psalter.[3] Most of our other psalters may be connected with these two families, and various attempts have been made at postulating unpreserved traditions. Such attempts lead, of course, to having to explain discrepancies uncovered by such studies, made as they must be, with limited materials.

The majority of the extant glossed psalters were given letter sigla by A. S. Cook, in his Biblical Quotations in Old English Prose Writers of 1898[4], and it is by these sigla that we now refer to them. Accordingly, scholarship in the editing of these Old English interlinear glossed psalters has generally been considered to be a product of the twentieth century. The early work was carried out in Europe between 1904 and 1914, and the later efforts began in 1959 as the projects of British and North American scholars. But such a restriction to the present century makes no provision for the fact that the earliest editorial interest in a glossed psalter was recorded in the seventeenth century, with the edition by J. Spelman of the Stowe Psalter[5] (designated F by Cook) in 1640. There was also a nineteenth-century edition made of the Vespasian Psalter (A) by Henry Sweet[6], who also published then the older glosses of the Blickling Psalter (M)[7] as well. E. Brock edited the later glosses of M between the years 1874 and 1880[8], and F. Harsley produced an edition of the singular Eadwine's Canterbury Psalter (E) in 1889.[9]

Six interlinear glossed psalters were edited by European scholars in the first two decades of this century. Briefly, these are the Regius Psalter (D), edited by F. Roeder in 1904[10]; the Junius Psalter (B), edited by E. Brenner in 1908[11]; the Cambridge Psalter (C), edited by K. Wildhagen[12], and the Arundel Psalter (J), edited by G. Oess[13], in 1910; and the Bosworth[14] and Lambeth[15] books (L and I respectively) edited by U. Lindelöf in 1909-1914. Four editions of glossed psalters have been published since the appearance of the much-delayed but exemplary text and commentary for the Salisbury Psalter (K) by Kenneth and Celia Sisam[16] in 1959. J. L. Rosier produced an edition of the fire-damaged Vitellius Psalter (G)[17] in 1962, which was followed in 1965 by Sherman Kuhn's new edition of the Vespasian Psalter[18], a project which was planned to include a supplementary volume of notes, as yet unpublished, although information from it has kindly been supplied by its author for this dissertation. The Vespasian Psalter has also been reproduced in facsimile form by David Wright, for the Early English Manuscript Facsimile series.[19] Liles re-edited Eadwine's Canterbury Psalter[20] in 1967, and most recently we have A. P. Campbell's edition of the hitherto-unpublished Tiberius Psalter (H)[21]. In preparation for publication is A. C. Kimmens' new edition of the Stowe Psalter[22], and at present, William Davey of the University of Ottawa is re-editing the Regius Psalter, and Frank Berghaus of Göttingen is at work on another edition of Eadwine's Canterbury Psalter.

To this list we should append the Paris Psalter[23], designated P, which was written ca 1025 in the southwest of England, and which consists of a parallel, rather than interlinear translation, the first fifty psalms in prose, and the last hundred in alliterating half-lines of verse. In Bodleian MS Junius 121, we find metrical psalm-verses in the Benedictine Office fragments[24] which display a similar, if not identical ancestry to that of the poetry of P. The common original, which is generally considered to be the work of one man[25], is in all probability a complete metrical psalter from which both derive. I have designated this proposed common original as V.[26] P itself has been edited in its several parts[27], and reproduced in facsimile form[28]; the Junius 121 metrical psalm verses have been collected by E. Dobbie as 'minor poems'[29] and are included in James Ure's compliation of the Old English Benedictine Office.[30]

There are a number of different methods and approaches associated with these editions of the interlinear glossed psalters described above. It is important to establish that no editor of any glossed psalter has given consideration to that approach with which this dissertation concerns itself. Similarly, no editor of these Old English metrical psalm-fragments has, to my knowledge, explored the possible relationship between vernacular glossed psalter traditions and vernacular psalm-based poetic paraphrase. The fundamental work which "lays the foundation of the study of gloss relations securely"[31] is U. Lindelöf"s critical examination, Studien zu altenglischen Psalterglossen.[32] This analysis has had a greater or lesser influence on every glossed psalter edition subsequent to it, but while it pioneers the study of inter-related glosses by a methodology not unlike that employed in this dissertation, it omits the related field of psalter-gloss and psalter-poetry collation.

Of the approaches of the early German editors, there is comparatively little to say. Eduard Brenner devotes the majority of his introductory comments to the technical questions of language, dating and provenance suggestions, and detailed manuscript description, and only turns his attention to the problem of inter-related psalter-glosses after completing this first survey. He cites Lindelöf in establishing the dependence of B on A:

> Das wichtigste Ergebnis seiner
> hieran geknüpften Untersuchungen
> ist die Feststellung der zwei-
> fellosen direkten Abhängigkeit
> unserer Glosse von der des Ves-
> pasian-Psalters.[33]

However, when dealing with the relationships of the other

psalter-glosses to the early <u>Vespasian</u> gloss, Brenner relies on Lindelöf entirely, and only generalizes in adding his own comments:

> Ausserdem bietet er von der
> Glosse der übrigen Psalmen alle
> von der des Vespasian-Psalters
> abweichenden Lesarten, "mit
> Ausnahme der rein graphischen
> oder morphologischen Varianten"
> . . . .[34]

Brenner's conclusions as to B's dependence on A are based on textual comparisons[35] and on a phonological analysis of the two glosses[36], but thereafter he returns to the question of B's date and origin, and approaches B's dependence on linguistic grounds, rather than on those which a comparison of A and B might suggest.

F. Roeder, who edited the <u>Regius Psalter</u> in the same year that Lindelöf produced his definitive study, provides an introduction similar to that of Brenner, which is mainly concerned with bibliographical details of date, provenance, and linguistic analysis. Like Brenner, he too generalizes about inter-relationships among the glossed psalters:

> Es liegt auf der Hand, dass ich
> in allen Fällen, wo mir Fehler,
> schiefe Übertragungen und überhaupt
> Schwierigkeiten aufstiessen, die
> übrigen glossierten Psalterien in
> möglichst ausgedehntem Masse zum
> Vergleich heranzog.[37]

However, unlike Brenner, he comments more specifically on singular traditions within the overall inter-relationship of the glosses, a first step towards the comprehensive examination of this question by Sisam, and one of the component elements of this dissertation: "Die Hss. ABC bilden eine ziemlich scharf hervortretende Gruppe, als deren Grundlage A anzusehen ist."[38] Roeder rightly sees D as at the heart of a tradition other than that of the A-type, and while his postulated DHK and FEGJ configurations have since been debated, nevertheless they mark what I have already termed a first step in an important aspect of glossed-psalter study.

We must note here that, in his edition of the <u>Cambridge Psalter</u>, Wildhagen lists variant readings to the C-gloss from other glossed psalters, his intention evidently being to obtain general groupings in accordance with Lindelöf's approach. Among the psalters which he uses[39], he includes readings from both the prose[40] and poetry sections[41] of the <u>Paris Psalter</u>, but seems to regard them as more of a curiosity than a valid psalter, since he makes no attempt to introduce P into any of the tentative groupings which he develops. However, because of this work, we should recognize that Wildhagen's psalter-gloss collation is significant, in that it has hitherto stood as the only exercise to include P in a group of glossed psalters. Nevertheless, Wildhagen fails to throw light on P's dependence upon a psalter-gloss, because his focus is centered on the C-gloss, to which, as we shall demonstrate, V bears a lesser, rather than greater relation.

To date, the most important glossed-psalter edition is the Sisams' <u>Salisbury Psalter</u>. This is so partly because of its accuracy of text, but chiefly because of its complete and valuable introductory material in the preface. While Sisam naturally discusses the standard bibliographical details common to any edition, he gives much of his commentary to the area of Lindelöf's <u>Studien</u>, and explores the interrelationships of the extant canon of Old English glossed psalters. It is essential at this point to recognize that although the <u>Paris Psalter</u> is itemized both in Sisam's bibliography of "psalters wholly or partly glossed in English"[42] and in his "list of extant psalters . . . written in England in Anglo-Saxon times"[43], the <u>Paris Psalter</u> is not included in his extensive study of such inter-relationships, nor does it appear in the later derivative lists for D where, as I plan to show, at least part of it belongs. Except for the indication that it has "a parallel translation"[44], P remains in Sisam's bibliography, unfortunately unexamined in the light of psalter-gloss traditions.

Starting with the assertion that "the scribe copied over his Gallican text a gloss ultimately derived from a Roman Psalter of the D-type, which we may call D^k"[45], Sisam examines the methods of glossing, spelling, and gloss language and vocabulary of K in terms of its dependence upon the postulated D^k source. He then cites Lindelöf[46] in re-affirming K's derivation from D, and begins his detailed analysis of psalter-gloss tradition in general, and more particularly, his study of both the D-type family and the <u>Regius Psalter</u> itself.

Sisam's conclusions about D are valuable for the
purposes of this dissertation, as well as for a deeper understanding of the Salisbury Psalter gloss. He makes distinct
reference to the prevalence in D of rare words and distinctive glosses[47]; he suggests that D itself is a copy[48], and
affirms that "MS Royal 2.B.v. is a book for study, not
a service book."[49] He discusses the evidence for D's
provenance[50], and finally approaches the important question
of D's connection with the earlier Vespasian tradition.[51]
He follows Lindelöf in concluding that "there is no good
evidence that type D is dependent on any other extant
gloss."[52]

Sisam then examines Lindelöf's results for derivatives
of D: the group of E (corrections), F, G, H, J, K, and L,
to which Sisam adds M and parts of I. As we have noted, the
metrical psalter V should be added in part to this derivative
group. It has, however, been excluded by Lindelöf, and
by Sisam after him. Working through this group, then, as it
stands[53], Sisam sets out suggestions of genealogy in the
following proposed stemmata:

1.

$$D^o$$
$$D^{gh}$$
$$H^d \qquad G^d, \ 54$$

where D^o is the original of the D-type gloss, D_d^{gh} the gloss
from which those parts of H and G derive, and H^d and G^d those
parts of H and G which are based on type D.

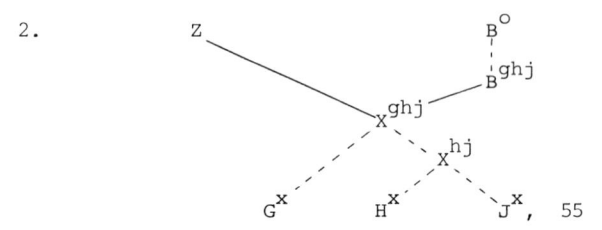

2.

$$B^o$$
$$B^{ghj}$$
$$X^{ghj}$$
$$X^{hj}$$
$$Z \qquad G^x \qquad H^x \qquad J^x, \ 55$$

where B^o is the original of a B-type psalter, B^{ghj} the gloss
from which the non-D (or "X") part of the GHJ grouping derives,
Z' may represent additions made at the beginning of a glossed
psalter"[56], and X and its derivative are the source for, and
embodiments of the non-D-type parts of G, H and J.

24

3.

```
                    D°
                  ⸝D fghj
              D gh⸝       ⸜D fj
           d⸝   ⸝d     d⸝   ⸜d
          H     G     J     F    ,  57
```

which explains in simple terms the inter-relationships
among psalters G (Vitellius), F (Tiberius), J (Arundel) and
F (Stowe), and their derivation from the original of the
Regius Psalter, D^o.

The stemmata in Figure 1, developed by Frank Berghaus
for his dissertation[58], provide an updating of both Lindelöf's
and Sisam's work. Briefly, A^o is the original for A; La and
Ea are those parts of L and E dependent upon the Vespasian
Psalter, while Ld and Ed are those parts dependent upon
the Regius Psalter; "Z" is as in Sisam, but "Y" is another,
now lost gloss tradition; D^1 and D^2 are the two "levels" of
glossing which Berghaus postulates; and Dro (identical with
D^1) and Dga are the extant Romanum (BL MS Royal 2.B.v.) and
a proposed Gallicanum text of D, respectively.

Naturally Berghaus slants his stemmata towards a
greater understanding of E which he is presently editing;
however, I have found his diagram to be the most complete
for my purposes, and I use it herein (with its author's
kind permission), to illustrate the psalter-gloss tradition
behind my chosen body of psalter-based Old English poetry.

Of the four later glossed psalter editions referred to
on page 21, I have little to say. As we have seen, Kuhn's
edition lacks a companion volume of notes, and neither
Campbell, nor Kimmens nor Liles, in their respective introductions, deals with the question of gloss relationship. In
his edition of the Vitellius Psalter, J. L. Rosier makes
reference to vernacular argumenta in the margins of G, which
unfortunately are fragmentary because of fire damage but
which are "similar, but not identical"[59] to marginal argumenta prefacing the prose psalms of the Paris Psalter.
Rosier relies on the collation of these scholastic inclusions
by Kenneth Sisam in Colgrave's facsimile of P^{60} to 'prove'
that "G's argumenta do not derive from P, and P cannot derive
its text from G."[61] Similarly, while quoting Sisam that
"there was no contact between the two manuscripts"[62], Rosier
does not exclude "the possibility of some form of distant
relationship, perhaps through a partial or complete recension

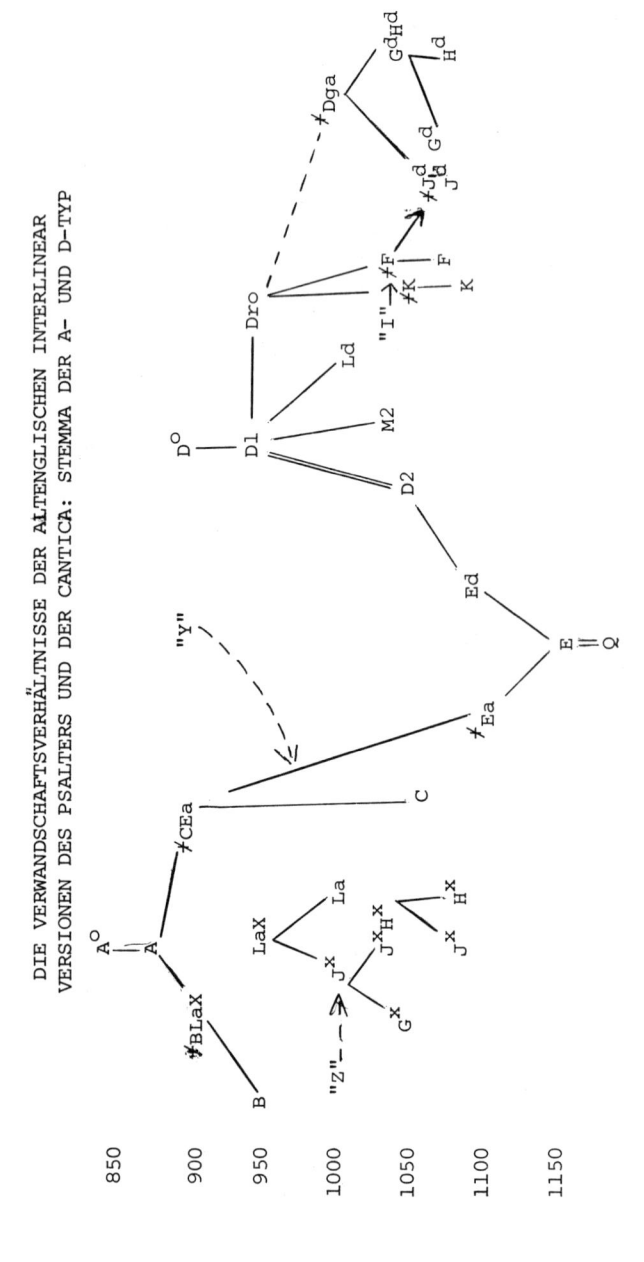

DIE VERWANDSCHAFTSVERHÄLTNISSE DER ALTENGLISCHEN INTERLINEAR
VERSIONEN DES PSALTERS UND DER CANTICA: STEMMA DER A- UND D-TYP

Figure 1

of P which was available at Winchester."[63] The relationship between G and the metrical parts of P, as viewed through the vernacular psalter-texts rather than marginalia, are to be included in the results of my collation of V with the Regius-type psalter-gloss.

Like the editors themselves of the interlinear glossed psalters, the scholars responsible for the various editions of V-fragments have uniformly ignored the possibility that their text derives from a specific psalter-gloss tradition. This would surely appear to be basic to such a study. To establish the evidence of a relationship between poetic paraphrase and prose translation is considerably more difficult than revealing a connection between gloss and gloss. But the aim of this dissertation is to bridge this vital gap in the study of both the Old English psalter and the Old English poetic paraphrase.

As I have shown, Kenneth Sisam includes the Paris Psalter both in his bibliography of vernacular psalters and in his list of extant Anglo-Saxon psalters, but he makes no further use of it, presumably either because the Paris Psalter has a parallel rather than an interlinear translation, or because two-thirds of it is in metrical form. Bertram Colgrave sets a terminus a quo of the years 959-991 within which to set the complete metrical ancestor of P, but while noting the quotation from it in the Cotton Tiberius B.i. poem Menologium[64], he hesitates to give a terminus ad quem other than a suggestion of the Benedictine Reform era.[6] This would tentatively place the composition of V in the period between 959 and 1000. During this same period of years, we see the appearance of the Regius, and perhaps of the Bosworth glosses, with the Vespasian, Blickling, and most recently, Junius glosses being already in existence and possibly acting as models. In addition to this, it is logical to assume that there was at least a prototype-C gloss extant at this time, bridging the gap between C and its original, the A^o gloss set out by Berghaus. Yet no editor of the metrical psalter fragments has considered that, in this productive period of Benedictine Reform, a relationship between a prose vernacular psalter and a metrical vernacular psalter might be just as likely as one between two prose psalters.

The Benedictine Office metrical psalm fragments have most recently been collected by James Ure, in a compilation of MSS Corpus Christi College, Cambridge 201 and Bodleian Junius 121. This compilation attempts to present as a whole

the extant version of this vernacular Office. Ure first
concentrates on the origins and dating of the two manuscripts,
and then gives over virtually the rest of his introduction
to the question of authorship. He suggests a date of composition for the vernacular Office manuscripts as being in the
mid-eleventh century, and gives an original composition date
of ca 1004-6 on the grounds of Fehr's dating of Ælfric's
first Old English pastoral letter to Wulfstan.[66]

> I attribute the prose parts of the
> text as we have them to Wulfstan,
> but consider that their original
> translation was the work of someone
> else, probably Ælfric, and that
> Wulfstan revised this translation,
> adding material of his own, and
> that he compiled the text by
> including a simplified adaptation
> of the monastic Office in use at
> Worcester and by incorporating
> the OE. metrical paraphrases and
> Psalm-verses.[67]

Yet, while Ure agrees with Thomson's popular proposal of the
existence of a complete metrical psalter (our V) as Wulfstan's
source[68], he ignores the question of where Wulfstan may have
found it. By his suggestion, then, a complete metrical
psalter must have been at Worcester ca 1000 for Wulfstan's
use in this 'compilation'. Ure also points out the connection between the Paris Psalter and the Benedictine Office
psalm-fragments. Then, after listing various critical
opinions on the date of V, Ure discusses for it a terminus
ad quem of the period 940-980 on the grounds of Bartlett's
dubious dating of the Menologium.[69] He eventually settles
for the general but incontestable observation that "the
composition of the metrical Psalms in P was considerably
earlier than the compilation of the Office."[70] Ure suggests
that the compiler of P fell back on V's metrical psalms when
his vernacular prose version gave out[71], but does not explain
the presence of metrical psalm-verses in the vernacular
Benedictine Office. To assume for no apparent reason that
Wulfstan included a metrical Old English version of psalms
where Ælfric omitted an Old English translation,[72] is surely
to underestimate Wulfstan. If Wulfstan is in fact the compiler, then the metrical psalms in the Old English Benedictine
Office must have been included with more intention than Ure
would suggest.

Nor does Ure amplify his suggestion that the Latin psalter-model for the Office is based on a 'Gallicanized' Bosworth-type psalter.[73] The Bosworth Psalter's Latin is Romanum, which in itself would make provision for the psalm-fragments, since these, like the psalms of P, follow the Roman text. The Bosworth Psalter is also of roughly the right period of compilation to support this, although it has been assigned to Canterbury.[74] While Lindelöf has established[75] that its gloss is in part dependent upon the D (Regius) tradition[76], Ure has omitted the vital step of collating his vernacular psalm-fragments with the Bosworth gloss to establish a definite pattern of influence.

It seems, therefore, to be a common trait among editors of Old English prose translations and poetic paraphrases alike, to ignore the potential connection between the metrical psalter and the psalter-gloss traditions. This may be a result of the mistaken assumption that all poetry was original and spontaneous. Even apart from the examination presented in this dissertation, the Paris Psalter is obviously derived from some vernacular source, since the V-poet is at times confused in his rendition of a verse[77]--perhaps when encountering difficulty in turning prose to meter--and yet, in other places writes his poetry with great facility. Such uneven style, when taken with the evidence which we have that his knowledge of Latin was inadequate for a direct composition[78], suggests that there was an intermediary stage between the Latin model and the finished paraphrase. What is more likely than a vernacular psalter-gloss? It is true that, when studying a poem like the Kentish Psalm 50[79], which contains its original Latin interspersed with its Old English translation, we are tempted to assume that the poet worked his composition directly from the Latin model. However, we must remember that a great many psalters, and in all probablility those most available to the monks, may have carried Old English glosses[80] which would, of necessity, have affected the composition of a poetic paraphrase based on their original text. These are considerations which have hitherto escaped the notice of scholars at work on the psalter paraphrase of the Old English metrical canon, and they open new doors on its origins.

It is my contention that the composition of V was in large part the result of liturgical influence, deriving from the two psalter-gloss traditions, the Vespasian (A) and Regius (D) families. As I have tried to show, the V-poet required an intermediate stage between his Latin text and his vernacular project, and I postulate this 'stage' as the

use of interlinear glossed psalters. I have every hope of
showing the extent to which he made use of each of the two
different gloss families, by means of the results of a
collation of the psalter-glosses described above, with the
V-fragments. Such results should shed light on the availability of the distinct gloss traditions for use in such an
undertaking, and on the possible co-existence of the two in
one scriptorium at one time. I would also hope that I may
assign the composition of our particular poetic paraphrase
to the period of the Benedictine Reform, perhaps as a byproduct of the movement, since the Psalms remain the foundation of the Opus Dei; and finally, I suggest[81] that this
complete metrical psalter was a work commissioned by a layman of some social influence, possibly the king himself.
This last proposal may therefore provide some insight into
the literary concerns of the court at Winchester.

The intention of this dissertation, therefore, is both
to trace the steps by which the influence of the glossed
psalter traditions may be systematically established in the
Old English metrical Psalter, and to tabulate the results of
such methodology in action, in order to get a clearer
picture of the relationships between V and the individual
codices (such as the Junius or Salisbury books), gloss
traditions (the A- or D-type psalter-glosses), or textual
variations (Romanum or Gallicanum texts).

I have chosen as a type-group for analysis a specific
number of glossed psalters to which I will refer below, and
certain sections of the Old English metrical Psalter as we
still have it. Since the Vespasian Psalter (A)[82] is at
least a century too early for our purposes, and since it may
have been held in high esteem[83] and therefore was probably
unavailable to scriptorium monks, it is unlikely to have
served as an actual model. However I have briefly examined
it as the closest original of the A-gloss psalters which we
still possess, and since Sherman Kuhn has proved, in his
unpublished notes for the companion volume to his edition of
A, that the Junius Psalter was copied directly from A.
Therefore, while I have neither subjected it to as rigorous
a collation as that set out below, nor tabulated extensive
results, I have included it as essential background for the
other psalters.

My first psalter-gloss used in the actual collation was
that of the Cambridge Psalter (C)[84] which, as Figure 1
suggests, represents one branch of the Vespasian tradition;

the other A-type branch finds its exemplar here in the Junius Psalter(B) already said to be a direct copy from A, which I examined after C. While C and B form a unit which may be seen to represent the Vespasian line, B was introduced to me with the Regius Psalter (D)[86], both being mid-tenth-century Romana which have been assigned to Winchester by Ker.[87] In working with D, I reached conclusions similar to those of Lindelöf and Sisam, these being that D is a singular psalter-gloss; that it was intended for educational, rather than liturgical purposes; and that it was a copy of a similarly-intended psalter from roughly the same part of England.

On the basis of these conclusions, I have postulated a date, a stemma, and a place of origin for BL MS Royal 2.B.v., and have uncovered a particular element in the manuscript which I call the 'Regius Ex Libris', and which has not been hitherto explained to my satisfaction.

In his edition of the Salisbury Psalter, Sisam suggests Worcester, Winchester and Canterbury as three possible provenances for the Regius Psalter. Worcester's case is based on the presence there in the seventeenth century of D's companion volume, BL MS Royal 4.A.xiv., which is not evidence enough to place Royal 2.B.v. in Worcester in the tenth century. Winchester's case is stronger, since we know that D was, in fact, at Winchester (probably in Nunnaminster 88) in the first half of the eleventh century.[89] Canterbury's case suggests that it is the latest, rather than the earliest medieval home of D, because of the partly-illegible late-eleventh century scribble on fol. 198v. This appears[90] to read:

>   . . . midne wintre ic scolde cuman
> ham þa axode (?)mon me hwæðer me
> wære leofre. . . . þar be wæsten
> . . .þonne on christes cyrcan ða
> sæde ic þæt me wære leofre on
> christes cyrcean þonne þar be
> westan swa hit æfre gewyrðe amen
> . . . .[91]

Briefly, then, I interpret ic to be, not the wandering ecclesiastic who inscribed a century-old (and therefore valuable) psalter with an unsigned note of praise for his own monastery, but boc itself. This is a riddle-like ex libris in which the Regius Psalter itself is the speaker.[92]

If this is the case, we may see that at midne wintre (probably at Christmas-tide) in the late eleventh century, the Regius Psalter was either brought from the west to Canterbury, or was being returned after a period of loan, to its library of that time (where its keepers doubtless felt that it belonged, swa hit æfre gewyrðe). We may therefore propose Winchester as being a major center to the west of Canterbury, from which D may have come. But whether MS Royal 2.B.v. was first brought from the west in the late eleventh century, or was returned after a loan, does not detract from its presence at Nunnaminster, Winchester, in the first half of the eleventh century. And while it could have originated in Canterbury and been loaned to Winchester where the first folios were added, we have no evidence to support such a conjecture. It is more likely that the book was written in Winchester, and subsequently translated to Christ Church, Canterbury.

This last proposal gives us both a date and a postulated stemma for the Regius Psalter. If D can be considered an educational book, it must be the product of a school, most probably of Benedictine monks. Before Æthelwold became bishop of Winchester in 964, no such school, to our knowledge, existed there. Thus we may more nearly pinpoint the generally-accepted composition date of ca 950[93], to a date shortly after 964. And if we assign the folio 7 prayer to ca 1025, it is possible to see the manuscript composed and added to in the same location, within a span of fifty or sixty years. To this proposal of date and provenance, we should now add the conjecture that D is a copy; hence we need an original (Sisam's D°) from the period before 964, from an area relatively nearby, and one which bears a gloss similar in purpose to that of D. I tentatively propose the following stemma:

        D°   written in Glastonbury
        | between 940 and 955
        |
        |
        |
        D   written in Winchester
             shortly after 964

since Æthelwold's Winchester settlement was founded by Abingdon and Glastonbury monks, and since Glastonbury was the earliest center of Benedictine Reform under Dunstan, 940-955.

With the study of D came singular results from my methodology of collation for the metrical psalter fragments; accordingly I chose for my final psalters, the Vitellius Codex[94] (G) as a member of what I term the "Winchester Gallicanum group"[95], and the Salisbury Psalter (K)[96], which seems unrelated to FGHJ. Both of these books are Gallicana, whose vernacular glosses appear to be the result of copying from a D-type Romanum psalter, and although they are both too late to have influenced V directly, they are used here to trace the line of descent from the Regius Psalter, as it might apply to a study of influence on the Old English metrical Psalter. From such an examination, I hope to be able to propose a genealogy for the metrical psalter, and eventually to examine the relationships, as they existed, among V, D, G, K, and peripherally, H (Tiberius), J (Arundel) and F (Stowe). While such a study would necessarily have to be reserved for an editorial examination of V, I have nevertheless included pertinent readings from all of the Regius books in Chapter III where they point up a particular tradition in the Old English metrical Psalter.

A collation between Old English psalter-glosses and Old English psalter-poetry presents considerable difficulty. Even before formulating a method of approach, it is evident that one must take into account the purposes and consequent limitations of psalter-gloss and of poetry, and that one must be prepared to qualify the results because of these limitations. The psalter-gloss is essentially a vernacular translation, and one must analyze its intention in order to understand its nature. As I have already tried to show, the Vespasian tradition seems to indicate a practical, liturgically functional purpose, while the Regius family stems less from this liturgical purpose than from an educational one. Yet this is not to suggest that psalters G, H, J, or F were meant to be no more than an exercise in translating Latin, or on the other hand that the B-gloss was nothing more than a translation of its Latin text for use liturgically. These two proposed attributes, liturgical and educational, should serve as indications of the nature of the Old English psalter-gloss and not as generic distinctions by which to classify them. From these suggestions, then, we can outline the restrictions of the psalter-gloss form as follows: it attempts to translate its Latin text into the vernacular literally, often using a double gloss where meaning is unclear or where two synonymous words might serve to render the Latin lemma more comprehensively than one. The latter case would suggest a less formal undertaking than that which gave rise to the initial use of the term 'continuous interlinear glossed psalter'. Nevertheless we are dealing with Old English prose which makes almost no attempt to follow any natural syntax, and which sets out to provide a word-for-word translation of the Latin psalter.

With Old English poetry, although very diversified in theme and content, one must again take account of its purposes and consequent limitations so that we may identify the specific elements which would be of use in our collation. The key to accomplishing this lies in recognizing the limits imposed by the metrical alliterative line. Although the poet who composed the complete metrical psalter set out to translate the Latin text with much the same intention as that behind the psalter-gloss, he was hampered by the very form he employed, since he depended on the use of words which had to fit into a stressed line, yet had to contain the essential elements for alliteration to provide those stresses. So, in such an undertaking, either translation or alliteration had to suffer, and unfortunately for our purposes, it was the alliteration. Critics[97] have suggested that the 'decaying alliteration' of the Paris Psalter is indicative of a late date of composition. I would prefer to regard this 'decaying alliteration' rather as the outcome of the conflict suggested above. But this is not to assume that the rules of metrical composition were relaxed for the writing of V.

Hence, in each pair of half-lines, the choice of one word by the V-poet would limit the choice of at least one other word (except in those instances where no alliteration is discernible at all). And since stress in an Old English alliterative half-line generally falls on words meant to stand out (the 'strong' parts of speech such as nouns, finite verbs and adjectives, which predominate in the Latin psalter-text), we may begin to understand the restrictions at work on the poet who attempted to turn such a text into an Old English psalter-poem. I have already proposed an intermediary stage, the vernacular psalter-gloss, on the grounds of the poet's lack of skill with Latin, and of the unavoidable influence of the gloss through its presence with its Latin text on the page used by the poet. I now suggest that such a stage was not only possible, but indeed very probable. It would be an essential source for the V-poet, which would either fortunately provide the appropriately alliterating translation, or at least would suggest a rendering for which he might find alliterating synonyms.

It is evident, therefore, that the conditioning factor between psalter-gloss and psalter-poem is language. The poet's choice of words is basic to his form, and, if I am correct in assuming an intermediary stage, that choice would be influenced by the vocabulary of the vernacular psalter-glosses. Syntax is a less effective basis for a collation methodology for, as we have noted, the syntax of the psalter-glosses follows for the most part[98] that of its Latin counterpart, while the psalter-poetry has to conform, as best it can, to the syntactical demands of alliterative meter. In neither case, therefore, do we find the free-flowing, natural syntax of regular Old English prose, but still the singular syntax of the gloss and that of the verse cannot be compared with any success.

Vocabulary, then, is our established basis, with the Latin text as the original common to both gloss and verse. Yet in many cases, the V-poet changes the sense of a psalm-verse, and the Latin lemma which has a corresponding translation in the glossed psalters will not appear as such in the Old English metrical version. Therefore I have primarily had to restrict my selection of lemmata to those which do, in fact, have translations in V which are comparable to the glosses of the psalters. Even so, the volume of possible lemma entries would make this work far too long; therefore, I have had to select only those lemmata which are not consistently rendered in one way in V, and which are strong (stressed elements and some particles) rather than weak (other particles and proclitics) parts of speech. I have concentrated on listing words which vary in translation in V and in the glosses, or which alternately show consistent accordances which in turn provide patterns for conclusions. For the most part I have also omitted those words which occur infrequently or which are rendered by the most common or obvious translation in both V and the psalter-glosses. Equally, I have not listed every instance of a commonly-occurring word being rendered in exactly the same way, as this would cause interminable repetition. As it is, many words recur in many of the psalm-verses, but I have tried to keep such redundancy to a minimum for the sake of conciseness.

Yet vocabulary to provide conclusions can cover a wide range of meanings, and for the purposes of this dissertation, we must distinguish between those elements which will be important and those which will not. Understandably, verb form in poetry will be as much the result of meter as of the poet's creative whim; therefore, unless it contains a specific

change (for example, from one person to another) which
affects the meaning of the verse, it should be ignored. Similarly, spelling, which is likely to be the result of dialect,
recopying, or both, should be discounted, as should the
presence or absence of the prefix "ge-". The aspects of
vocabulary which will form the foundation of our collation
conclusions used here, will comprise the renderings of a
lemma which are particular to the metrical psalter and to
one psalter-gloss family; those mistranslations which are
common only to the poem and to a sole gloss tradition; and
similarly-common textual renderings which, if not errors in
translation, are at least the result of erroneous interpretation of grammatical form and of what punctuation we are
able to determine or postulate.

    With these aspects of vocabulary in mind, I have
formed a tabulation process which will make provision for
virtually all possible combinations of accordance. With the
'X' lists covering those readings in V which show alliteration in two half-lines, and the 'Y' lists compiling those V
readings which show no alliteration, I propose the following
format on which to base both my resulting tabulation, and my
commentary on it:

> Lists 1X and 1Y cover readings in which V accords
> with the Vespasian tradition (the Junius and
> Cambridge books, B and C), but not with the
> Regius tradition (the Regius, Vitellius and Salisbury
> books, D, G and K respectively). Sublists 1X-C, 1Y-C
> 1X-B and 1Y-B contain readings in which V accords
> with one of the Vespasian psalters only.
>
> Lists 2X and 2Y cover readings in which V accords
> with the Regius and not the Vespasian tradition.
>
> Lists 3X and 3Y cover readings in which V accords
> with both the Regius and Vespasian traditions.
>
> Lists 3X1 and 3Y1 cover readings in which V accords
> with the majority of the four type-glosses used
> here[*]; the tradition behind V is noted in each case.
>
> Lists 4X and 4Y cover readings in which V accords
> with neither the Regius nor the Vespasian tradition.

[*] K has not been included as a type-gloss per se, since it
carries a singular vernacular translation, which is undoubt-

edly of the Regius-family, but remains unpredictable as a tradition representative. However, I have recorded K's readings throughout, and shall discuss it more fully in my conclusions.

Thus we may see the formulation of a methodology of collation as follows: the establishment of what might be termed vocabulary 'ranges' for the chosen glossed psalters and the poetic psalter paraphrase; the analysis of these ranges in terms of lemma renderings, mis-translations, and erroneous interpretations outlined above; and the tabulation of significant similarities and of traditions apparent in the materials collated, as described in Lists 1XY through 4XY.

With the foregoing in mind, I have developed a methodology which is not unlike that of Lindelöf in his Studien zu altenglischen Psalterglossen. However, I have based my collation on the following model, in consideration of the fact that the Latin text in its two versions is definitely common to both the poetry and the psalter-glosses:

Latin lemma = psalter gloss rendering, poetic rendering

for example,

dominus = dryhten O, hlaford V

where O is the siglum representing the specific psaltergloss, and V denotes the metrical psalter's reading. I have also noted where a gloss in a Gallicanum psalter may follow the Romanum text, by indicating the alterations from Roman to Gallican format where they occur in the original Latin.

In keeping with my selection of lemmata for the sake of confining such a study to the limits of a dissertation, I have chosen certain psalms from each glossed psalter for collation with the metrical psalter fragments. Since the Paris Psalter poetry begins part-way through Ps. 51, I have initially chosen a 'run' of twenty psalms (51-70) to provide basic vocabulary ranges for each psalter-gloss and for V. Thereafter, for the purposes of examining the relationship in other parts of the psalter, I have chosen liturgically-important psalms which are said once a day in the Benedictine Office, rather than once a week. These are Mattins Psalm 94, Lauds Psalms 148, 149 and 150, and Compline Psalm 133.[99] Of these remaining daily psalms, Lauds Psalm 50 is preserved in prose form in P, as is the second Mattins Psalm 3, and

and Lauds Psalm 66 is already included in the initial vocabulary range 'run'. This procedure gives us twenty-five metrical psalms, from approximately one hundred, for our collation of P itself with the psalter-glosses. The selections are spaced in numerical order, with roughly twenty, forty and ten intervening psalms.

```
51————————— 70——————————94——————————133————148——150
50 ————————— 75——————————100——————— 125 ——————————— 150
```

The Benedictine Office psalm-fragments present no such problem, for their selections are short enough, and indeed few enough in number to allow for collation with all the psalm-verses included in Bodleian MS Junius 121. It is true that some of the selections are identical to verses already collated in the psalter-gloss/<u>Paris Psalter</u> comparison, but these have been re-collated to preserve the unity of the group. To maintain clarity in the exercise, I have not included the variant readings from MSS Cotton Tiberius B.i. and Trinity College, Cambridge R.17.i.

I have accordingly compiled the Junius 121 psalm-fragments and the <u>Paris Psalter</u> selection in numerical order, noting any variant readings from the Benedictine Office verses which fall within P's vocabulary 'run'. By organizing my metrical materials in this way, I have tried to piece together the remains of V, as we have them, thus considering the original metrical psalter as a single piece for almost the first time.[100]

It is perhaps of importance to note that the Benedictine Office psalm-fragments are in fact V in action, for the collection of these verses, taken from the complete metrical psalter, provides functional prayers: the preces, versicles and responses of the canonical Hours. The opening versicle for each Office is 69:1, which we find repeated seven times in Junius 121. Thereafter, almost all of the remaining psalm-verse selections accord with their proper Offices, thus:

> <u>Prime</u>: 86:13, 70:8, 50:9-12, 139:1, 58:1-2, 60:8, 64:5, 102:1-5, 84:4, 32:22, 19:9, 27:9, 121:7 and 101:1.
>
> <u>The Capitular Office</u>:[101] 115:6, 89:16-17, 123:8.
>
> <u>Terce</u>: 40:4, 89:13.

<u>None</u>: 18:12

<u>Vespers</u>: 140:2, 123:8, 140:2, 40:4

<u>Compline</u>: 84:4, 16:8

Compared with a modern ordinal, this gives us virtually the whole of Prime, but only short selections from the Capitular Office, Terce, None, Vespers and Compline, with no inclusion at all from Lauds or Sext. Yet we still have remaining in Junius 121 vv. 53:1, 43:27, 118:175-176, 5:1-4, 24:1-4, 34:1-3, 122:22, 50:1 and 79:9, all under the aegis of Prime, without an obvious place in the Office. However, since I have not extended my study to include an examination of a breviary or similar ordinal contemporary with the Tenth Century Reform, I must assume that the medieval Office of Prime contained as preces, certain psalm-verses which have since fallen into disuse. These psalm-selections from Junius 121 have also been collated on the same model,

$$\text{latin} \leq \text{gloss, poem}$$

and have been appended to the P-selections as described above, to provide an overall view of the dependence of V on the psalter-gloss traditions. I have tabulated the results according to the format already described, and have compiled the proposed lists and provided commentary on them, to establish evidence on which I have based my conclusions.

NOTES

1. Kenneth and Celia Sisam, eds., The Salisbury Psalter (E.E.T.S.242: 1959), p.75.

2. BL MS Cotton Vespasian A.i: Romanum text from 8th[C] and gloss from last quarter of 9th[C].

3. BL MS Royal 2.B.v.: Romanum text and gloss from the third quarter of the 10th[C].

4. A. S. Cook, Biblical Quotations in Old English Prose Writers (London: 1898), xxvii ff.

5. BL MS Stowe 2: Gallicanum text and gloss ca 1050-1075. Ed. J. Spelman, Psalterium Davidis Latino-Saxonicum vetus (1640).

6. H. Sweet, ed., The Oldest English Texts (E.E.T.S. o.s. 83: 1885), p.183 ff.

7. Morgan Library, New York MS M.776: Romanum text late 8th[C], scattered glosses. Contemporary glosses ed. H. Sweet, Ibid., p. 122 ff.

8. Complete gloss ed. E. Brock in R. Morris, ed., The Blickling Homilies (E.E.T.S. 58, 63, 73: 1874-1880), p.251 ff.

9. Trinity College, Cambridge MS R.17.i: parallel Romanum Hebrew and Gallicanum texts and gloss ca 1150, gloss to pss. 90:15-95:2 copied from V or a recension of V. Ed. F. Harsley, Eadwine's Canterbury Psalter (E.E.T.S. o.s. 92: 1889). Also in facsimile, M. R. James, The Canterbury Psalter (1935).

10. F. Roeder, ed., Der altenglische Regius-Psalter (Studien zur englischen Philologie 18. Halle: 1904).

11. Bodleian MS Junius 27: Romanum text and gloss ca 925. Ed. E. Brenner, Der altenglische Junius-Psalter (Anglistische Forschungen 23. Heidelberg: 1908).

12. Cambridge University Library MS Ff. 1.23: Romanum text and gloss ca 1025. Ed. K. Wildhagen, Der Cambridger-Psalter (Bibliotek der ags. Prosa 7. Hamburg: 1910).

13. BL MS Arundel 60: Gallicanum text and gloss ca 1050-1075. Ed. G. Oess, Der altenglische Arundel-Psalter (Anglistische Forschungen 30. Heidelberg: 1910).

14. BL Additional MS 37517: Romanum text and partial gloss ca 1000. Glossed psalms ed. U. Lindelöf, Die altenglischen Glossen im Bosworth-Psalter (Mémoires de la Societé néophilologique de Helsingfors 5. Helsingfors: 1909).

15. Lambeth Palace (London) MS 427: Gallicanum text and gloss ca 1025. Ed. U. Lindelöf, Der Lambeth Psalter (Acta Soc. Scient. Fennicae 35.i and 43.iii. Helsinki: 1909-1914).

16. Salisbury Cathedral MS 150: Gallicanum text ca 975, gloss ca 1025, Ed. K. and C. Sisam, The Salisbury Psalter (E.E.T.S. 242: 1959).

17. BL MS Cotton Vitellius E.xviii: Gallicanum text and gloss ca 1050. Ed. J. L. Rosier, The Vitellius Psalter (Cornell Studies in English 42. Ithaca: 1962).

18. Sherman Kuhn, ed., The Vespasian Psalter (Ann Arbor, Michigan: 1965).

19. David Wright et al, eds., The Vespasian Psalter (Early English Manuscript Facsimile 14. Copenhagen: 1967).

20. Bruce Liles, ed., "The Canterbury Psalter: An Edition with Notes and Glossary", (Stanford diss.), DA 28, (1967), 1053A.

21. BL MS Cotton Tiberius C.vi: Gallicanum text and gloss ca 1050-1075. Ed. A.P. Campbell, The Tiberius Psalter (Ottawa: 1974).

22. A. C. Kimmens, ed., "An edition of the British Museum MS Stowe 2: The Stowe Psalter" (Princeton diss.), DA 30 (1969), 1139A. TBP by the Toronto Old English Series.

23. Paris Bibliothèque Nationale MS Fonds Latin 8824: Romanum text and parallel translation in prose (pss. 1-50) and verse (51-150) ca 1025.

24. Fols. 42-53v of Bodleian MS Junius 121.

25. First suggested by E. Thomson, *Godcunde Lar 7 Þeowdom: Select Monuments of the Doctrine and Worship of the Catholic Church in England before the Norman Conquest* (London: 1849), and thereafter generally accepted.

26. See page 4 for assignment of V as a provisional siglum, V designates "verse" for the Old English metrical Psalter, and the sub-sigla Vp, Vj, Ve and Vm denote the mss. where fragments of V remain.

27. Hitherto ed. B. Thorpe (1835); C. W. M. Grein in *Bibliotek der angelsächsischen Poesie* (cf. note 41); B. Assmann in *Die Handschrift von Exeter, Metra des Boetius, Salamo und Saturn, Die Psalmen* (*Bibliotek der angelsächsischen Poesie*, herausgeben von Richard Paul Wülker 3 Band. Leipzig: 1898), pp. 332-476. Also numbered 2nd part, pp. 86-230; J.W. Bright and R.L. Ramsay, *Liber Psalmorum: The West Saxon Psalms* (Boston: 1908); and G. P. Krapp, *The Paris Psalter and the Meters of Boethius* (A.S.P.R. V. New York: 1932).

28. Bertram Colgrave et al, eds., *The Paris Psalter* (E.E.M.F. 8. Copenhagen: 1958).

29. E. Dobbie, ed., *The Anglo-Saxon Minor Poems* (A.S.P.R. VI: New York: 1942).

30. James Ure, ed., *The Benedictine Office: An Old English Text* (Edinburgh: 1957).

31. Sisam, *The Salisbury Psalter*, x.

32. U. Lindelöf, *Studien zu altenglischen Psalter-glossen* (Bonner Beiträge 13. Bonn: 1904).

33. E. Brenner, *Der altenglische Junius-Psalter*, xi.

34. *Ibid.*, xi.

35. *Ibid.*, xii-xv. These, and the examples covered in note 36 are undoubtedly dependent upon Lindelöf"s collations.

36. *Ibid.*, xv-xxxiii.

37. F. Roeder, *Der altenglische Regius-Psalter*, xx.

38. *Ibid.*, xxi.

39. These being A (ed. Sweet); B (ed. Brenner); D (ed. Roeder); E (ed. Harsley); F (ed. Spelman); L and I (ed. Lindelöf); J (ed. Oess); and G, H, and K, still unedited in 1910.

40. He refers to James W. Bright and Robert L. Ramsay, eds., Liber Psalmorum: The West Saxon Psalms.

41. He refers to Christian W. M. Grein, ed., Bibliotek der angelsächsischen Poesie, 2 Band (Göttingen: 1858), pp. 147-276 and ff.

42. Sisam, The Salisbury Psalter, ix.

43. Ibid., pp.47-48.

44. Ibid., p.75.

45. Ibid., p.17.

46. Ibid., p.39; and Lindelöf, Studien zu altenglischen Psalterglossen, pp.121 ff.

47. Sisam, pp.39-40.

48. Ibid., pp.42, 54-55.

49. Ibid., p.52

50. Ibid., p.53-54.

51. Ibid., 55-56; this particular question has vexed scholars of psalter-gloss study for decades, and the opinions range from definite assertions that no connection exists, to an equally adamant certainty of influence. This dissertation takes the conflict into account, but under no circumstances tries to prove or disprove the influence of the Vespasian gloss on that of the Regius psalter.

52. Sisam, p.56.

53. Ibid., pp.56-75.

54. Ibid., p.62.

55. Ibid., p.66.

56. Ibid., p.64.

57. Ibid., p.71.

58. Frank Berghaus, Die Verwandschaftsverhältnisse der altenglische interlinear Versionen des Psalters und der Cantica (Göttingen diss.), TBP by Palaestra.

59. J. L. Rosier, The Vitellius Psalter, xvii.

60. Bertram Colgrave et al, eds., The Paris Psalter (E.E.M.F. 8), p.16.

61. Rosier, xvii-xviii.

62. Ibid., xvii. No Sisam reference for the Colgrave facsimile of The Paris Psalter is given in Rosier.

63. Rosier, xviii.

64. Menologium, ll. 60-62, quotes three lines from V''s Psalm 117:22. However, dating for this poem is uncertain and only ll. 42b-44a, which refer to St. Benedict (and thereby, perhaps, to the Benedictine Reform of ca 963) give any indication of its era of composition.

65. Colgrave, The Paris Psalter (E.E.M.F. 8), p.17.

66. B. Fehr, Die Hirtenbriefe Ælfrics in altenglischer und lateinischer Fassung (Bibliotek der ags. Prosa 9:1914), liii.

67. James Ure, The Benedictine Office, p.25.

68. Ibid., p.44.

69. H. Bartlett, "The Metrical Division of the Paris Psalter" (Baltimore: Johns Hopkins diss., 1896).

70. Ure, p.19.

71. Ibid., p.19.

72. Ibid., p.44.

73. Ibid.,p.24.

74. Lindelöf places it between 975 and 1000 in his edition of L; for the assignment of L to Canterbury, cf. P. M. Korhammer, "The Origin of the Bosworth Psalter" (Anglo-Saxon England 2 (1973), pp.173-187.

75. cf. Lindelöf, ed., Die altenglischen Glossen im Bosworth-Psalter.

76. From which, as we shall see later in this dissertation, the metrical psalter family is partly derived.

77. cf. Psalm 54:19 in The Paris Psalter.

78. cf. errors discussed later, in Ps. 59:5 of V. That these errors are present in Junius and Regius also is not as significant here as the evidence of the V-poet's inability to translate Latin with any great ease.

79. BL MS Cotton Vespasian D.vi., fols. 70-73v.

80. Sisam, The Salisbury Psalter, p.75.

81. Along with Colgrave, in his facsimile of The Paris Psalter, and in accordance with the suggestion made to me by Milton McC. Gatch on the occasion of our tentative assignment of V to Winchester. The evidence for his suggestion is contained in Mechthild Gretsch's "Æthelwold"s translation of the Regula Sancti Benedicti and its Latin Exemplar" (ASE 3 (1974), p.125.

82. Sherman Kuhn, ed., The Vespasian Psalter (1965).

83. If we are to believe Thomas of Elmham. David Wright, in his facsimile of A (Copenhagen: 1967) calls it a "luxury service book".

84. K. Wildhagen, ed., Der Cambridger-Psalter (1910).

85. E. Brenner, ed., Der altenglische Junius-Psalter (1908).

86. F. Roeder, ed., Der altenglische Regius-Psalter (1904).

87. N. Ker, A Catalogue of Manuscripts Containing Anglo-Saxon (Oxford: 1957), item 335 (B), pp.408-409; and item 249 (D), pp.318-320.

88. And hence Sisam, The Salisbury Psalter, p.53.

89. A prayer included on the later-added folio 7 invokes the aid of Nunnaminster's patron the Blessed Virgin, its first abbess and the saint whose cult was popular there as in other Winchester churches.

90. I have followed Sisam, The Salisbury Psalter, p.53, but have checked his reading against both a transcript made for me by William Davey, and a photograph of the original folio.

91. I have expanded some forms, including 'xo' to 'christes', after Sisam.

92. For further study in this, cf. my article "The Ex Libris of the Regius Psalter", presently in preparation.

93. Ker et al.

94. J. L. Rosier, ed., The Vitellius Psalter (1962).

95. A group composed of psalters G (Vitellius), H (Tiberius), J (Arundel) and possibly F (Stowe).

96. K. and C. Sisam, eds., The Salisbury Psalter (1959).

97. G. P. Krapp, ed., The Paris Psalter (1932), xvii et al.

98. B shows syntactical inversions in the second half of the psalter, but these generally consist of only two words, often compound verbs.

99. A lacuna in B forbids the examination of these three Lauds psalms.

100. It is treated as a unity, although only a small selection of psalms is dealt with, in Benno Tschischiwitz's dissertation, Die Metrik der angelsächsichen Psalmenübersetzung (Breslau: 1908).

101. Consisting of the reading of the martyrology, followed by a brief Office of versicles, responses, collects, the Gloria patri, Kyrie eleison, Pater noster, and a blessing.

Chapter III: Tabulation and Results

Before providing the collation lists with their introductions and commentaries, I consider it necessary to discuss the alliteration of V briefly, and to clarify certain aspects of these tabulations and notes, which might be confusing without explanation. First, it is important to notice that I have confined my textual sources for V to Krapp and Dobbie, eds., The Anglo-Saxon Poetic Records, volumes V; and VI, pp. 82-86. From these editions of Vp and Vj, I have used both the psalm verse numbers and the variant readings for V, but have not followed the Latin text as it appears in Dobbie. For a more accurate version of the Latin lemmata and for psalm verse numbering in the glosses, I have referred to the interlinear glossed psalters themselves. By this arrangement for V, one may see in the commentary the following format: 'read beorhtnes in Krapp, p.61'. This means that the psalm-verse in which the entry is found is one of the Vj fragments also preserved in Vp, and that the form taken from Krapp in A.S.P.R. V differs in some fashion from the form taken from Dobbie in A.S.P.R. VI. I have relied upon Dobbie's readings throughout Vj, but have added any variant readings from Krapp in this way in the appended commentaries.

Some of the terminology used in the actual commentaries requires advance explanation. The expression 'singular', found throughout my notes, refers only to singularity among the five psalters collated, or between the two recognized psalter-gloss traditions. While a gloss may in fact preserve a reading which is unique in the whole canon of glossed psalters, I have not distinguished it as such from a reading which is unique only with respect to the other psalters used in this dissertation: any other approach would make the task of commenting on the tabulation lists unnecessarily complicated. Hence, 'singular' is a relative term in these commentaries, and should be treated as such. The phrase 'K and G follow the Ga. text' refers to the glosses of the two Gallicanum psalters, Salisbury (K) and Vitellius (G), adhering to their proper Latin original. If the Gallican lemma is in any way comparable to the Roman lemma it replaces, I have added the emended Gallican reading in parentheses after the Romanum entry, and have indicated in the gloss in K or G where necessary. However, in those places where the Gallican text differs so greatly from the Roman that the lemma has no visible counterpart and there is no indication of a vernacular Romanum reading, or even a gloss which might approximate a Romanum reading in K or G, I have simply noted 'K and G follow the Ga. text'. Since the Latin basis for this study is the Romanum and not the Gallicanum psalter, I have considered it unnecessary to add these substantially-different emendations to the Latin text.

Before considering lists based on alliterative restriction, something should be said about the alliteration in V. Although the meter of V is, generally speaking, freer than that of Beowulf, it can, and has been discussed in terms of the Sievers" five types.[1] I have used this previous work as a guide in my treatment of V's alliteration.

There are in V a number of patterns of alliteration which do not appear in the meter of Beowulf: 's' alliterates with 'sc', 'sw', 'st' and 'sn'; 'w' alliterates with 'wr' (52:1), and, most interestingly, 'hr' alliterates with 'r' (101:20). Double alliteration and internal and end rhyme are fairly common. My own assignment of V-readings to the alliteration or non-alliteration lists is therefore naturally subject to opinion. I have based my choice not only on a scansion of each half-line of verse, but also on precedent set elsewhere in V.

The following collation lists and their commentaries are set out as follows:

Example:

43:27(26)   adiuva   fultum V: gefultuma CBA
                                    gefylst DG; andfylst K

This format can be explained in simple terms: the numbering to the left of the entry, which forms a column down the left-hand side of the page, represents the psalm-numbering. 43:27(26) here denotes that the lemma adiuva is from Psalm 43, verse 27 in V, but verse 26 in the interlinear glossed psalters. The double-numbering of the verses is to be expected, since the V-poet did not confine himself to the specific numbering of the glossed psalter texts. The word which follows, and forms the next column on the page, is the Latin lemma itself. In some cases, a second lemma, prefixed by 'Ga.' will follow it in parentheses: this is the variant Gallican reading, which is included wherever it occurs. The Old English entries are then divided into the V-reading, and the glossed-psalter-readings. The V-reading will show the alliterating element in each word for the 'X' or alliterative restriction lists, by having the pertinent letter underlined; as above, fultum shows us an 'f'-alliteration for that line in V. The psalter-gloss readings are set out such that, for

50

the Vespasian/V accordances, the Vespasian readings are on the same line as the V-readings, while the Regius readings are on the line below; this should facilitate the comparison of accordances in examining the lists. Similarly, for the Regius/V accordances, the readings from the Regius psalters are on the same line as that from V, while the disagreeing Vespasian readings are on the line below. For the lists in which both the Vespasian and Regius psalters accord with V. the line below has been used where extra space for the readings is needed. The denotation lacuna for a glossed psalter (abbreviated lac) means that part of the manuscript is missing or illegible; the term unglossed (abbreviated ungl) means that the lemma stands without a gloss in that particular psalter.

The notation ≠ before V-readings in the alliterative restriction lists (the 'X'-lists) designates instances in which a double alliteration occurs in the line of poetry containing the reading. And while this does not constitute a case for the suspension of alliterative restriction, it nevertheless should be noted if alliteration is to be regarded as a criterion for classification. For those attempting to scan the half-lines of this poem, I would also caution that, while alliteration may appear between two half-lines, this does not always guarantee that both of the half-lines will agree with one of Sievers' Five Types. For example, in Psalm 68:15(16), puteus is rendered seað in V (line 2a of that verse) which alliterates with supe in line 2b: however, 2b is an A-type line, but 2a has been identified by Tschischiwitz as relating to a "/x/" pattern, and hence belongs by his account to none of the Five Types.

Collation Lists 1X and 1Y

Collation Lists 1XY tabulate those readings in V which accord with the Vespasian(A) and not the Regius (D) glossing tradition. Naturally, those readings on the Y-list, that is, those words in V whose choice by the poet was not restricted by alliteration requirements, are more to our interest, as there is no apparent reason for their presence in V, other than that of direct influence from a Vespasian-type psalter. In the case of the readings in the X-list, the poet may have rejected the Regius glosses as alliteratively unsuitable, and perhaps turned to the Vespasian books for a synonym for a lemma which did alliterate.

Once again, I should list the psalters used in this dissertation: the Junius (B) and Cambridge (C) books represent the Vespasian family, and the Regius (D), Salisbury (K) and Vitellius (G) books represent the Regius family. Yet, while K is technically a Regius book, it is not part of a identifiable Regius-type family such as the Winchester Gallicanum group like G, and it preserves a large number of readings which are either singular among the five psalters studied here, or which accord with V when no other psalter-gloss does. For this reason, I have included K for comparison purposes only; it shall be dealt with more comprehensively in my conclusions. In addition to this, while we can safely consider both B and C as representative of an A-tradition in equal measure, we should pay closer attention to D than to G for the preservation of the Regius-type gloss. This is the case for two reasons: G is a fire-damaged manuscript and, in many places, lacks part or all of a gloss because of marginal crumbling at the edge of a folio, which occurrences I have noted. G, too, is one of the two Gallicanum psalters used in this study and, more than does K, exhibits a tendency to follow the Gallican text. G often preserves a double, or even a triple gloss, but unlike the double glosses of D, those in G often represent both the Vespasian and Regius traditions. Hence, to set out the list for clarity:

A: Vespasian Psalter; Vespasian tradition: probably not a direct influence but collated where specific readings are necessary.

B: Junius Psalter; Vespasian tradition: quite possibly a direct influence, as gloss is from ca 925.

C: Cambridge Psalter; Vespasian tradition: too late for a direct influence (gloss ca 1025) but examined for a prototype-C gloss influence on V.

D: Regius Psalter; Regius tradition: quite possibly a direct influence, as gloss is ca 964.

K: Salisbury Psalter; Regius tradition: too late for a direct influence (gloss ca 1025) but examined for a prototype-K gloss influence on V.

G: Vitellius Psalter; Regius tradition: too late for a direct influence (gloss ca 1050-1075) but examined as a member of the Winchester Gallicanum group for a prototype -FGHJ gloss influence on V.

Collation Lists 1X-C, 1Y-C, 1X-B and 1Y-B

Collation sublists 1XY-C and 1XY-B tabulate those occurrences in which V accords with only one of the Vespasian-type psalter-glosses, but not the other, and not the Regius family. For each entry, I have noted the reading in the Vespasian Psalter itself to determine lines of influence more clearly.

Collation Lists 2X and 2Y

Just as Collation Lists 1XY tabulated readings in which V accorded with the Vespasian and not the Regius tradition, so Collation Lists 2XY provide those readings in V which follow the D and not the A family. I have devoted a greater amount of attention in my comments for these lists than to those of Lists 1XY, since the accordance between the V and Regius readings is not as immediately apparent as that between V and the A family. I would attribute this fact to the proposed nature of the D-gloss, i.e., that of an educational, rather than a liturgical translation, and hence would consider the obscurity because of the number of errors preserved in D. Therefore, while an agreement between V and the Regius family on an error gives us substantial proof of direct influence, I have provided detailed comments in such cases to clarify this proof for the reader.

Collation Lists 3X and 3Y

Collation Lists 3XY tabulate the surprisingly large number of readings in which V accords with both the Vespasian and Regius traditions. This once more opens the question of Vespasian influence on the Regius gloss, and perhaps the results of these lists may provide more evidence for the solution to the problem. Naturally, a commentary on lists of such accordance will be slight: therefore I have concentrated on technicalities of what may be metrical importance in V, and on peculiarities of textual adherence and singular reading in the psalter-glosses for the majority of my notes.

Collation Lists 3X1 and 3Y1

These lists serve as a "holding tank" into which may be put readings which do not conform with the initial pattern of the Collation Lists. In each case, we find a singular reading in at least one of the four type-psalters (B,C,D, or G), while the other three generally accord with the reading found in V. However, I should here draw critical attention to the difficulties presented by G which I have already mentioned before.

It often preserves compound glosses for a lemma, and in many cases its double gloss will represent both the A and D traditions. I have included in these two lists only those reading sets from G which are both singular and notably different from the readings in C, B, D or V.

In discussing Lists 3X1 and 3Y1, I shall compare the readings from A with singular glosses in C and B, and readings from F (Stowe), H (Tiberius) and J (Arundel) with singular readings in D and G. I have again included K readings but would again note that K is not used here as a type-psalter because of its unique glossing vocabulary; hence any singularity in K does not play a part in the classification structure for these two lists.

Collation Lists 4X and 4Y

There is naturally a large percentage of readings in which a poetic paraphrase does not accord with its prose translation source. These readings have been tabulated in Collation Lists 4XY. In my commentary to List 4X, I have included an indication of the alliterative elements in V, where a discussion on V's choice of an independent reading is pertinent; in List 4Y, which is virtually self-explanatory I have confined my comments for the most part to peculiarities in the glossed psalters. It is interesting to note the extent to which the Vespasian and Regius traditions differ; I have not drawn attention to all cases but, as in previous lists, I have noted the textual tradition (Ro. or Ga.) behind the psalter-gloss readings.

Most of the V-readings in these two lists are figurative interpretations, and should perhaps be viewed as creative rendition, despite the obvious attempts to conform with metrical or alliterative requirements. Although each entry deserves comment, I have restricted myself to those which require amplification, explanation, or which are not readily comprehensible to the reader.

NOTES

1. B. Tschischiwitz, Die Metrik der angelsächsischen Psalmenübersetzung (Breslau: 1908). Tschischiwitz notes a sizeable number of half-lines which belong to no specific 'Type', and hence which are exceedingly difficult to read aloud.

COLLATION LIST lX

5:1(3)	intende	beheald V: CB, behald A begym DK, lac G
24:3(4)	fac	⁺do V: CB, doo A ungl D, not in K or G
24:3(4)	semitas	stiga stapas V: stige CB sið fatu DK sið fatu/stige G
24:5(6)	miserationum	miltsa V: myldsa CB miltsunga/ofearmunga D mildsunga K (ge)miltsung(æ) G
34:1(2)	inpugnantes	þa..fuhtan to V: onfeohtyndan C, on- fehtendan B onwinnende DKG
43:27(26)	adiuva	fultum V: gefultuma CB gefylst DG, andfylst K
51:6(9)	adiutorem	fultum V: CA, fultumiend B gefylsten DG, lac K
52:3(3)	filios hominum	manna bearn V: bearn manna CBA suna manna DKG
54:4(5)	cecidit	fealleð V: gefeoll CA, feoll BK hreas DG
54:5(6)	contexerunt	beþeahton V: beþehton CB bewrigon D and so K, bewreah G
54:10(11)	plateis	weorþige V: wurðigum C, worðignum BA strætum DG, feldan K
54:10(11)	usura	mansceat V: wæstmsceatt CB, westem- sceat A gestreon DKG
54:22(24)	puteum	seaðes V: seað CBA pytt DKG

55:1(2)	tota die	ealne dæg V:	CB, alne deg A
			ealne dæi K
			ælce dæg DG
55:4(5)	sermones	wordum V:	word CB
			spræca D and so KG
56:3(4)	obprobrium	edwit V:	CB
			hosp DK, hosp/on edwit G
57:4(5)	obdurantis	dytteð V:	fordyttynde CB
			forelyccende DK
			forcliccende G
57:4(5)	surde	deafe V:	C, deaðe B
			ungl D, dumbe KG
57:7(9)	cecedit	feallað V:	gefeol CBA
	(Ga. supercecedit)		hreas D, oferhreas KG
58:3(4)	fortes	strange V:	BK, stronge CA
			þreafulle DG
58:9(10)	fortitudinem	strengðe V:	strengo CA, strenge B
			strengð K
			strangnisse DG
58:11(12)	destrue	toweorp V:	BG, towurp C
	(Ga. depone)		tobrec DK
58:12(13)	superbia	oferhygde V:	oferhigde C and so BA
			ofermodinesse DKG
58:13(14)	finium terræ	eorðan gemæru V:	gemære eorðan CB
			ende eorðan DKG
58:17(18)	adiutor	fultum V:	CBA
			gefylstend DKG
59:1(3)	repulisti	todrife V:	adrife CB
			anyddest DK, eart G
59:1(3)	destruxisti	towurpe V:	CBA
			tobræce DKG
59:6(9)	Effrem	Effrem V:	CBAG
			wæstmbærnis DK
59:7(10)	Idumea	Idumea V:	CBA
			eorðlican þing DK
			þa eorðlican G

61:2(3)	adiutor (Ga. susceptor)	fultum V: CB	andfenge D, gefylstend KG
61:4(5)	honorem (Ga. pretium)	are V: CB	weorþunga D, wyrð K, weorð G
61:12(12)	potestas	miht V: meaht CB	anweald DKG
62:6(6)	exultationis	wynnum V: wynsumnysse CBA	upahefednisse DG upahafenesse K
63:3(5)	sagittent	scotian þenceað V: scotodon CBA	scotian K strælian D and so G
63:5(7)	scrutati sunt	smeagað V: smeagynde C and so BAG	scrunadon DK
64:1(2)	votum	gehate V: CBA	gelast D, behæs K gelast/gehat G
64:1(2)	decet	gedafenað V: B, gedafynað C, gedeafenað A	geriseð DK, gehreoseð G
64:7(8)	sustinebit	aræfnan V: arefnyð C, aræfneð B, arefneð A	acymð D, not in K or G
64:12(12)	benignitatis	fremsumnesse V: B and so CA	medemnisse DKG
65:3(4)	adoret	geweorðie V: wurðiað C and so BA	wyrþiað K gebiddað DG
65:10(11)	dorso	bæce V: CB hricge DKG	
65:11(12)	refrigerium	colnesse V: colnysse CA, edcoelnisse B	rotnesse/frofer DG rotnesse K

65:14(16)	narrabo	s̱ecgean wylle V:	secge C, seccgeo B, secgo A cyðe DKG
67:1(2)	oderunt	⁂f̱eodan V:	CB hatedon DKG
67:2(4)	epulentur	habbað s̱ymbel V:	symbliað CBA gewistfullien D and so KG
67:10(10)	perfecisti	gef̱remest V:	gefremdyst C and so B fulfremedest DKG
67:10(10)	segregans (Ga. segregabis)	ascadeð V:	tosceadynne C, tosceadende BA asyndriende DK, syndrast G
68:3(4)	laboravi	w̱ann V:	C, ḻac B, won A swanc DKG
68:8(8)	reverentia (Ga. confusio)	hleorscame V:	mid sceame CBA forwanndunge DK gescyldnes G
68:8(8)	improperium (Ga. obprobrium)	edwit V:	CB hosp DK edwit/hosp G
68:14(14)	luto	ḻame V:	CB fenne DKG
68:14(15)	odientibus (Ga. qui oderant)	f̱eondum V:	B, feogyndum C hatiendum DK þa þe hatedon G
68:15(16)	puteus	s̱eað V:	CBA pytt DKG
68:17(19)	velociter	hṟædlice V:	CB, hredlice A raðe D, hraðe K hrædlice/widlice G
68:19(29)	verecundiam (Ga. reverentiam)	arsceame V:	s̱ceame C and so BG forwandunge DK
68:20(21)	improperium	heaṟmedwit V:	edwit CBA ungḻ D, hosp KG

68:30(31)	cantico	lofsange	V: C, sange BK cantice DG
69:1(2)	ad adiuvandum	gefultuma	V: to gefultumianna C and so BA to fylstanne DKG
69:2(3)	revereantur	scame dreogað	V: scomiyn C, on scunigen BA forwandien DKG
69:2(3)	confundantur	beoð gescende	V: gescynde C and so BA gescamigen DKG
69:6(6)	adiuva	gefultuma	V: CBA gefylste DKG
70:6(7)	prodigium	forebeacen	V: B, forebiecn C foretacen DKG
70:6(7)	adiutor	fultum	V: CA, fultumiend B gefylstend DKG
70:15(16)	potestas	mihte	V: C, mehte B, mæhte A anwealde DKG
70:18(18)	potentiam	mihtes þrym	V: mihte CB, mæhte A anweald DKG
70:19(20)	abyssis	neowelnesse	V: nywulnysse C and so BA grundum DG deopnesse K
70:20(21)	exortatus (Ga. consolatus)	hulpe..getrymedest	V: trymmende CBA lærdest DK gefrefrodest G
94:2(2)	iubilemus	singan mid wynne	V: wynsumiyn CB drymen DG lac K
94:4(3)	repellet	wiðdrifeð	V: adrifyð CBA anydeþ D, not in K or G

94:9(9)	probaverunt	c͟unnedan V:	cunnodon BA fandodon/cunnydon C fandodon DKG
148:7(7)	abyssi	n͟eowel͟nessa V:	nywilnysse C and so A l͟ac B grundas DKG
149:4(4)	beneplacitum	w͟el licendlic V:	welgelicod C l͟ac B gecweme DK gecwemedlic G
149:8(8)	alligandos	b͟indan V:	bindannæ C, gebindenne A l͟ac B gewriþene DKG
150:2(2)	potentibus (Ga. virtutibus)	h͟eahmihtum V:	mi͟htum C, l͟ac B anwealde DK mægenes G

COLLATION LIST 1X-C

51:8(11)	fecisti	gew͟orhtest V:	worhtyst C, l͟ac BK dydes A, dy̅dest D dy(..) G
52:1(2)	corrupti sunt	ons͟ceoniendlice V:	onscuniyndlice C l͟ac K gewemde A and so BDG
56:10(9)	diluculo	æ͟rmergene V:	ærmorgyn C, ærmargen A in dægred B, ondægred DG on dæire K
59:6(9)	manases	g͟leaw Mannases V:	gleaw C Manasses ABDKG
139:1(2)	libera (Ga. eripe)	gen͟ere V:	C, nera K(G) alies BD gefrea A

140:2(2)	incensum	r̲ecels V:	recylsum C
			inbernisse A, onbærning B,
			onbærnesse G
			anal D, an store K

COLLATION LIST 1X-B

59:5(8)	Siciman	S̲iciman V:	BA
			þa mægðe C
			byrðen DKG
59:7(10)	Allophili	A̲llophilas V:	BA
			sigelhearwan C
			lease cristene DK
			ælfremede G
64:1(2)	in Sion	in S̲ion V:	BA
			on Sion/on lifes sceawunge C
			on heahnisse DKG
67:2(2)	fumus	r̲ece V: B, rec A
			smic CDKG
70:2(2)	libera (Ga. salva)	al̲ys V:	alies B
		u̲ngl D	
		gefreo CA	
		gehæl KG	

COMMENTARY FOR COLLATION LIST 1X

24:3(4)   f̲ac: this is probably not strictly a Vespasian indication in V, since D is unglossed, and K and G follow the Ga. text.

24:3(4)   s̲emitas: G's double gloss represents both the A and D glossing traditions.

24:5(6)   m̲iserationum: both the A-reading m̲yldsa and the D-reading m̲iltsunga provide V with the proper alliterating consonant for the line; therefore, alliterative restriction is not a deciding factor here in V's use of the Vespasian tradition.

43:27(26)   adiuva: as with miserationum, 24:5(6), either the
            A- or D-reading would have provided V with the
            right "sound": hence V's choice of the Vespasian
            over the Regius reading is significant.

51:6(9)   adiutorem: cf. note on miserationum, 24:5(6)

52:6(9)   filios hominum: this reading, as it is shown in
            the entry in V, the A-family, and the D-family,
            is repeated throughout the Psalter in each case
            wherever these lemmata are found together. V
            appears to invert the word order for metrical
            reasons.

54:10(11)   plateis: K preserves a singular reading.

56:3(4)   obprobrium: G shows a double gloss of both the
            A and D traditions.

57:4(5)   obdurantis: forcliccende in G may be a scribal
            error.

57:4(5)   surde: deaðe in B is a scribal error for deafe

57:7(9)   cecedit: note that K and G follow the Ga. text
            supercecedit with oferhreas as opposed to the
            simpler hreas for the Ro. text in D.

58:3(4)   fortes: K accords with the A-family.

58:9(10)   fortitudinem: K follows the A tradition here.
            Note that in V the first consonantal unit "st"
            makes up the alliterating element for the line,
            while it is elsewhere alliterated with "s" by
            itself. Cf. also note on miserationum, 24:5(6).

58:11(12)   destrue: G follows both the Ro. text and the
            Vespasian family.

58:12(13)   superbia: Tschischiwitz has identified the half-
            line containing this translation in V as a "C"
            type, hence it is the prefix "ofer" and not the
            substantive "hygde" which takes the alliterative
            stress here.

58:13(14)   finium terræ: note that V is essentially not under
            alliterative restriction to accord with the A fam-
            ily, since it is eorðan which takes the allitera-

tor stress, rather than gemæru. In fact, the D family's reading ende would have provided V with a third alliterating word in the line.

58:17(18) adiutor: cf. note on miserationum, 24:5(6).

59:6(9) Effrem: here in D, as elsewhere, we find a suggestion of etymological glossing, possibly for homiletic commentary rather than for liturgical purposes. This etymological interpretation is found in many of the Regius-family psalters as well.

59:7(9) Idumea: cf. note on Effrem above for etymological interpretation of names in D.

61:2(3) adiutor: K and G follow the Ga. text, susceptor.

61:4(5) honorem: D appears to follow the Ga text pretium, as opposed to the Ro. text which is clearly rendered as are in the Vespasian family. K and G follow D's reading weorþunga with similar translations.

63:3(5) sagittent: K follows the A tradition.

63:5(7) scrutati sunt: G accords with the Ro. text and the Vespasian family gloss.

64:1(2) votum: G preserves both the A and D readings.

64:1(2) decet: G preserves a singular reading here.

65:3(4) adoret: K follows the A tradition.

65:11(12) refrigerium: the error in D (the double gloss is probably due to the scribe reading refugium for refrigerium) is duplicated in G. K repeats only the first gloss in D, rotnesse.

67:10(10) segregans: G follows the Ga. text segregabis with syndrast, while K follows the Ro. text with asyndriende.

68:8(8) reverentia: G probably follows the Ga. text either with an original translation, or after a lost Ga. gloss tradition, with gescyldnes, unique from the A and D gloss reading.

68:8(8)	improperium: also in 68:10(11), obprobrium: these are most commonly glossed edwit in the Vespasian family and in V, and hosp in the Regius books. But note the double gloss in G in 68:8(8), preserving both readings.
68:14(15)	odientibus: G follows the Ga. text qui oderant, but K follows the Ro. text.
68:17(19)	velociter: the double gloss in G preserves the A reading and another, unidentified tradition which does not accord with D.
68:19(29)	verecundiam: the V reading here is part of a lost line, hence no alliterating element is shown for the entry. G. follows the A gloss.
68:30(31)	cantico: note the Latinate in DG, K follows the A tradition.
69:6(6)	adiuva: cf. note on miserationum, 24:5(6).
70:6(7)	prodigium: cf. note on miserationum, 24:5(6), since the stress falls on the "f" of forebeacen, not on the "b".
70:19(20)	abyssis: K preserves a singular reading.
70:20(21)	exortatus: G follows the Ga. text while K follows the Ro. text.
94:4(3)	repellet: K and G follow the Ga. text.
94:9(9)	probaverunt: note the unusual double gloss in C, preserving both the A and D readings.
150:2(2)	potentibus: G follows the Ga. text while K follows the Ro. text. V adds "heah" to "mihtum" to provide for alliteration.

COMMENTARY FOR COLLATION LIST 1X-C

51:8(11)	fecisti: this is not strictly a singular indication for C, as B preserves no gloss for this lemma.

However, I have included it here as A differs from
C with dydes, which also appears in D and G.

52:1(2) corrupti sunt: V and C accord, while B, D and G
follow the Vespasian reading.

56:10(9) diluculo: V agrees with C and A, while B accords
with the Regius family.

59:6(9) manases: V reads gleaw Mannases, with the first
stress on "g", while manases is glossed as a
proper name only in ABDKG. C alone preserves the
singular reading gleaw from which part of the
V-rendering may have been taken.

139:1(2) libera: the two Gallicanum psalters K and G, whose
text reads eripe, follow genere in V and C, while
A preserves its usual gloss of gefrea, and B and
D preserve their usual gloss of alies. This
entry is interesting since C commonly accords with
A for this lemma. It is possible that we see a
Gallican textual influence here in both V and C,
since elsewhere in Romanum texts the gloss genere
for the lemma eripe and not libera is very common.

140:2(2) incensum: C and V accord alone, while A, B and G
agree, and D and K each preserve a singular reading. (read ricels in Krapp, p.137).

COMMENTARY FOR COLLATION LIST lX-B

59:5(8) Sicimam: the proper name appears as the gloss
in V, B and A, while C preserves a singular
reading which is interpretive, and the D-group
preserves another unique reading which is either
an error in translation or interpretive as well.
Sicimam appears to alliterate with samod of
59:5(5b), although its own line, 5a, belongs to
no identifiable type of scanned line.

59:7(10) Allophili: as with Sicimam, V, B and A render the
lemma as a proper name, while C stands alone, as
does G, D and K accord in what appears to be an
etymological interpretation.

64:1(2)   in Sion: V, B and A preserve this as a proper
          name, C double-glosses the lemma with the A-
          reading first and perhaps an interpretive trans-
          lation second, and the Regius family glosses
          in Sion as on heahnisse, probably from an
          etymological tradition.

67:2(2)   fumus: V, B and A accord, while C follows DKG.

70:2(2)   libera: this may not in fact be a singular
          accordance between V and B, since D (which
          usually glosses libera as alies) is here unglossed.
          Yet it is interesting to compare this entry with
          libera in 139:1(2), since here A and C agree on
          gefreo, which is the gloss most commonly found in
          both throughout the Psalter to translate libera.
          K and G follow the Ga. text salva with gehæl.

COLLATION LIST 1Y

53:4(6)   adiuvat   fultumeð V: gefultumige C, geful-
                                      tumeð BA
                                      gefylsteð DK
                                      gefylsteð/gefultumiað G

54:10(11) defecit   aspringe V: asprong BCA
                                      geteorade DK, georade G

54:11(13) oderat   feodon V: feode CB, fiode A
                                    hatude DKG

54:16(18) narrabo   sæcge V: secge CB, seggo A
                                   cyðe DKG

55:3(4)   debellant   feohtað V: ofyrfeotað CB
                                     oferwennað D, not in K
                                     or G

55:6(7)   inhabitabunt on eardiað V: oneardigeað C and so
                                      BK, in eardiað A
                                      eardiaþ DG

55:6(7)   expectavit   bad V: BA, gebad C
           (Ga. sustinuerunt)   anbidode DK, geþyldegodon G

66

55:9(11)	sermonem	word V:	CB
			spræce DKG
55:10(12)	vota	gehat V:	CBA
			gewilnunga DG, behæsa K
55:10(12)	placeam	licode V:	gelicige C, licige B,
			licie A
			cweme DKG
56:12(11)	nubes	wolcnum V:	CB, wolcnu A
			genipu/lyfta D, lyfte K,
			genipu G
57:8(10)	priusquam	ærðon V:	CB
			ærþam DKG
58:6(8)	circuibunt	ymbgað V:	B, ymgað C, ymbgað A
			ymbyrnað DKG
58:8(9)	deridebis	dest..to bysmre V:	bismrast CB
			and so G
			hyspest DK
59:6(8)	fortitudo	strengþu V:	streng CB
			strangnes D and so K
			strangnes/strængð G
59:9(12)	reppulisti	drife V:	awegadryfe C, adrife BA
			anyddest DKG
60:1(2)	deprecationem	bene V:	beny C, boene BA
			halsunga DG, gebed G
60:2(4)	turris	tor V:	BA, torr C
			stypel DK, stypel/torr G
61:8(8)	auxilii	fultum V:	fultumes BA, fultumys C
			fylstes DKG
63:4(6)	sagittabunt	scotiað V:	scotydon C and so BA
			stræliað DG, scotiaþ K
63:7(8)	parvulorum	cilda V:	CBA
			lytlinga DKG

65:17(19)	intendit (Ga. adtendit)	beheold V:	behealdyð C, behaldeð B, bihaldeð A gegymð D, begymð K, begym G
67:21(22)	conquassavit	gescæneð V:	CBA tocwysde D, tocnysde K gescæneð/tobracð G
67:23(25)	ingressus	gangas V:	gongas C, ingong (gongas) B on stæpas DKG
67:27(31)	concilium	gemot V:	A, lac B geþeaht/gemot C geþeaht D gemot/gaderung G gegæderung K
68:9(10)	ceciderunt	gefeollon V.:	gefeollun CA, feollon B hruran DK, lac G
68:16(17)	benigna	fremsum V:	CBA medeme DG, welwyllenda K
68:20(21)	expectavit	gebad V:	C, bad BA anbidode DG, anbidiað K
68:36(36)	adquirunt	begytað V:	C, begitað B, bigeotað A secað DKG
68:36(36)	possedebunt	gesittað V:	BA, gesetteð C agun DK, agnedon G
69:3(4)	erubescant	scamien V:	scamiyn C and so BG areodigen D and so K
69:4(4)	erubescentes	sceamien V:	scamiende CBG aryderende D, reodiende K
70:1(1)	confundar	weorðe gescended V:	gescynd C and so BA gescamige DG forwyrðe K
70:9(10)	dixerunt	cwædon V:	CB, cwædan K, cwedun A sædon DG

70:12(13)	confundantur	beoð.. gescende V: gescynde C and so BA
gesceamigen DKG
70:14(15)	pronuntiavit	sægeð V: sægð CB, segeð A
cyþde DK, deð riht G
70:16(17)	pronuntiabo	sægde V: forþsecge C and so BA
cyþe DKG
70:17(18)	adnuntiabo	asecge V: secge CBA
bodige DKG
94:10(10)	proximus	neah V: neawyste C and so BA
gesyb D, not in K or G
118:175	adiuvabunt	fultumiað V: gefultumiað CBA
fylsteð DKG
133:4(3)	fecit	worhte V: CB
dyde DK, dyde/worh(..) G

COLLATION LIST 1Y-C

58:15(16)	murmurabunt	gnorniað V: CA
geomriað B
murcniað DKG
68:4(5)	oderunt	feogeað V: feodon C, fiodun A, <u>lac</u> B
hatedon DKG
68:9(10)	obprobria
exprobantium	edwita V: edwit edwityndra CA
hospas edwitendra B
hospas hyspendra D
hospas hyspende K
hospas/edwit hospendra/tal-
lendra G
70:15(15)	negotiati-
ones
(Ga. litteraturam)	ceapunga V: ceapunge C
scire A and so B
gestreon D, <u>ungl</u> k
stæfgefeig G

149:3(3)   in choro   on ðreatum V: mid þreate C, in
                                         ðreate A
                                         lac B
                                         on choro DKG

COLLATION LIST 1Y-B

24:6(7)   ignorantes   uncuðe V: unondcyðignesse BA
                                    nytyndnysse C, nytyn-
                                    nysse DG, nytenyste K

COMMENTARY ON COLLATION LIST 1Y

54:10(11) defecit: georade in G is the result of faulty
           copying from a D-type psalter.

55:6(7)   expectavit: G follows the Ga. text sustinuerunt.

55:6(7)   inhabitabunt: V accords more with the A tradition
           which provides a prepositional prefix, than with
           the D tradition which simply reads eardiaþ. Note
           that K accords with the A family.

55:10(12) vota: K preserves a singular reading.

56:12(11) nubes: D preserves a double gloss, of which K
           copies the second element, and G the first.

58:8(9)   deridebis: G accords with the A family.

59:6(8)   fortitudo: G preserves both the A and D readings.

60:1(2)   deprecationem: K preserves a singular reading.

60:2(4)   turris: G preserves both the A and D readings.

63:4(6)   sagittabunt: K preserves the A reading in accord-
           ance with V.

67:21(22) conquassavit: tocnysde in K is a scribal error for
           tocwysde in D. G preserves both the A reading and
           a unique gloss which does not accord with D.

67:27(31) concilium: gemot in V accords with A: C and G both double-gloss this lemma with gemot as one element, but in the C-translation the second gloss element agrees with geþeaht in D, while in the G-translation the second gloss element accords with gegæderung in K, and is probably the result of the Ga. text, congregatio.

68:9(10) ceciderunt: G's lacuna is due to fire damage at the edge of fol. 68v.

68:16(17) benigna: K preserves a singular reading.

69:3(4) erubescant: also 69:4(4), erubescentes: G follows CB instead of DK.

70:9(10) dixerunt: K follows the A tradition in accordance with V.

70:12(13) pronuntiavit: note the error in G, deð riht, but for pronuntiabo, 70:16(17), G glosses the lemma correctly as cuþe after D.

94:10(10) proximus: K and G follow the Ga. text.

133:4(5) fecit: G preserves both the A and D readings in a double gloss which is partly illegible due to fire damage.

COMMENTARY ON COLLATION LIST 1Y-C

58:15(16) murmurabunt: V accords with C and A, while B preserves a singular reading, and DKG agree together.

68:4(5) oderunt: this may not necessarily be an indication of V and C in singular accordance, since A agrees with their gloss reading, and B is unglossed. However, I have listed it for convenience.

68:9(10) obprobria exprobantium: of the confusing selection of glosses for this double lemma, only C and A preserve edwit edwityndra, which accords with the simplified edwit in V. B retains edwitendra for <u>exprobantium</u>, but follows the D-gloss in <u>hospas</u> for <u>obprobrium</u>. D and K accord with <u>hospas hyspendra</u>, while G double-glosses each element of the lemma, the first with the A and D readings, and the second with the D reading and a singular reading, <u>tallendra</u>.

70:15(15)   <u>negotiationes</u>: V and C agree in a singular reading, while A and B accord with <u>scire</u>. D's influence is hard to trace here, as K has no gloss and G follows the Ga. text, <u>litteraturam</u>.

149:3(3)   in <u>choro</u>: like <u>oderunt</u>, 68:4(5), this may not necessarily be an indication of singular accordance between V and C, since the last part of the Psalter is not preserved in B. A accords with V and C, and DKG preserve a Latinate reading, on <u>choro</u>.

COMMENTARY ON COLLATION LIST 1Y-B

24:6(7)   <u>ignorantes</u>: V accords with B and A, while C accords with the <u>Regius</u> family.

COLLATION LIST 2X

34:1(1)	nocentes mei	d̠eredon V: deriende D and so KG sceðþyndan C and so B
34:3(3)	dic	s̠æge V: sege DKG cweð CB
52:6(6)	sprevit	forh̠ycggeað V: forhygede DG, <u>lac</u> K forhogode CB
54:5(6)	timor et tremor	e̠gsa me 7 fyrhtu V: ege 7 fyrhto/ bifung D ege 7 fyrhto K ege 7 bifung C

		ege 7 cwacung B
		ege 7 gryre/bifung G
54:7(9)	pusillo animo	m̱odes m̱indom V: medmiclum mode D lytyllmodum C and so B medmiclum gast K and so G
54:7(9)	tempestate	m̱ægenes hreoh V: hreohnisse DK heortnesse G storme CB
54:11(13)	absconderem	ẖyde V: hydde DK ahydde G behydde CB
54:16(18)	adnuntiabo	ḇodie V: bodige DKG cyðe CB
56:10(9)	cythara	ḫearpe V: hearpsweg D and so K hearpan G cythere C, ungl B
58:12(14)	consumma- tionis	on e̱nde V: geendunge DG, ungl K gefyllydnysse C and so B
59:5(8)	letabor	ḇlissie V: blissige DKG beo geblissod CB
59:5(8)	metibor	M̱etiboris V: unglossed as for other proper names in this psalm DKB metui AG amete C
61:4(5)	cucurri in sitim: ore suo benedicebant	urnon/ḇurstige muðe V: ic arn on ḇurst of muðe DK arn on dust of muðe G orn on ðurst his muðes bledsadon A arn on þurst muðe hys bletsodan C arn on ðurst mid muðe mira hie bletdoson B

73

64:4(5)	tabernaculis (Ga. atriis)	earduncgstowum V: eardungum D and so K ungl G geteldum CB
64:14(14)	hymnum	lofe V: lofsang DKG ymen CA, ymensong B
65:1(2)	dicite	*segeað V: secgað DG cweðaþ CBK
65:4(5)	terribilis	egeslice V: egeslic DKG egysfull C and so BA
65:11(12)	transivimus	farað V foron DKG eodan C, leordan B
67:12(13)	spolia	weorðlic read V: reaflac DKG heryreaf CB
67:25(28)	duces	latteow V: latþeowas DG, laðþewas K heretogan CA, lac B
68:2(2)	tempestas	hreoh V: hreohnis DK and so G storm CA, lac B
68:14(15)	eripe	alys V: DKG genere CB, gere A
70:22(24)	confusi	scende V: gescynde DKG gedrefyd CB
89:15(13)	aliquantulum (Ga. usquequo)	hwæthwygu V: hwætwega D hu lange KG sume hwile CB
148:9(9)	cedri	cedrum V: cederas D and so G cedertreu K cedyrbeam C, lac B
149:3(3)	psalterio	psalterio V: saltere DKG hearpan C, lac B

COMMENTARY FOR COLLATION LIST 2X

52:6(6)   sprevit: the "forhy" part of the reading in V and DG provides the alliteration: "forho", which begins the CB reading would therefore not do, although the actual verb is the same.

54:5(6)   timor et tremor: tremor, translated as fyrhtu, is unusual. Therefore, it is important to notice that the alliterating word here is egsa in V, rather than fyrhtu which accords with the first element of D's double gloss, and with K. Alliteration is therefore not a deciding factor in V's choice of the individual D reading. C and B each renders tremor differently, while G double-glosses it, according first with a singular reading and then with the C-gloss.

54:7(9)   pusillo animo: perhaps the "m" sound in D suggested the "m" alliteration in V: however, animo is glossed mode in D with no adjectival prefix as in CB, and V similarly renders it modes. K and G read gast for animo.

54:7(9)   tempestate: it is the modifier mægenes and not the noun hreoh which alliterates in V. Hence, as in timor et tremor, alliterative restriction is not imposed on V's choice of DK over CB. The G reading heortnesse is probably scribal error for hreohnisse.

54:11(13) absconderem: V follows the simplex form hydde in DK rather than the complex ahydde in G or behydde in CB

59:5(8)   letabor: V accords with the form of DKG rather than that of CB.

59:5(8)   metibor: rendered Metiboris, a proper name, in V, this lemma is left unglossed, as for a proper name, in D, K, and surprisingly, B. Since Psalm 59 has many proper names of unfamiliar origin which are left unglossed in D, I must assume that the Regius glossator read metibor as a proper name as well. It should however be noted that the form metibor is an anomaly, and is therefore unfamiliar to any glossator who might expect metiar

instead. The error may have originated with a
scribe who read letabor in the same psalm-verse,
and rendered what should have been metiar as
metibor through visual duplication of endings.

61:4(5) cucurri in sitim: ore suo benedicebant: this
reading depends on an error in punctuation. V,
D and K assume that sitim and ore go together,
pointing to a misunderstanding of the Latin text.
G reads dust for ðurst, perhaps scribal error or
perhaps mistranslation, while A, B and C
"punctuate" correctly, although the Latin text
itself is an awkward rendering of the Hebrew.

65:4(5) terribilis: egeslice in V has the stress on the first
"e": hence the suffix "lice", which follows DKG,
rather than the suffix "ful", after ABC is not
under alliterative restriction.

67:12(13) spolia: weorðlic reaf in V, with the alliteration
on "w", is closer to reaflac in DKG than to the
complex heryreaf of CB.

89:15(13) aliquantulum: V and D show singular accordance
while K and G follow the Ga. text usquequo. (read
hwæthwiga in Krapp, p.61).

148:9(9) cedri: V accords with the simplex cederas of DG,
rather than cedertreu in K or cedyrbeam in C.

149:3(3) psalterio: although V preserves a Latinate form,
it accords with the anglicized saltere of DKG,
rather than hearpan of C.

COLLATION LIST 2Y

5:1(3) voci orationes min gebed V: stefne gebedes DKG
                                  stefne gesprecys CB

55:10(12) reddam   gylde V: K, agylde DG
                               agyfe C and so B

57:4(6)	venefici	wið attrum V:	ætrene D, ættrene KG
			gealdorcræftas C and
			so B
58:3(4)	occupa- verunt (Ga. ceperunt)	ofþryhtun V:	ofþrycton D, þrihtan K, ungl G ofyrsetton C abisgodon B
58:6(7)	convertantur	gecyrrað V:	gecyrrad D and so KG sien forcyrryde C and so B
58: 6(7)	patiantur	þoliað V:	þolien D and so KG þrowiyn C and so B
58:14(15)	convertantur	gecyrrað V:	gecyrrede DKG forcyrryd C, forcirde B
60:6(8)	reddam	agylde V:	DKG agyfe C, agife B
64:1(2)	reddetur	gylde V:	bið agolden DK, aguldon/agifen G byð agyfen C and so B
65: 1(2)	iubilate	herian V:	herigað D and so K heriað/wynsumiað G wynsumiað CB
65:2(3)	dicite	secgeað V:	secgað DG cweðað CBK
67:2(3)	defecit	geteoriað V:	teorade DG, geteorade K asprong CB
67:8(8)	transgrediens	ferað V:	færst DKG ofyrgæst CBA
70:1(2)	libera	alys V:	DKG gefreo CBA
70:20(22)	cythara	hearpan V:	DG, hærppan K cithan C, citran B

COMMENTARY FOR COLLATION LIST 2Y

57:4(6)   venefici: C and B preserve an independent reading not shared by V or the Regius Family.

58:3(4)   occupaverunt: C and B each preserve a singular reading, while V accords with DK and G is left unglossed.

58:14(15)   convertantur: C and B have the prepositional "for" instead of the simple prefix "ge" as in V, D, K and G.

64:1(2)   reddetur: the alliteration is very obscure in the two half-lines where this reading appears in V, but I have construed it as an "h"-sound, falling on Hierusalem and gehate, such that the palatal "gy" of gylde is unaffected. This is, however, debateable.

65:1(2)   iubilate: G preserves both the D and A traditions in a double gloss.

65:1(2)   dicite: K follows the A tradition, cf. also in List 2X, ps. 65:1(2).

70:20(22)   cythara: C and B preserve Latinate readings cithan and citran, not shared by V or the Regius family.

COLLATION LIST 3X

5:3(5)	videbo	geseo V:	CBDKG
19:9(10)	domine	drihten V:	CBDKG
19:9(10)	fac	do V:	CBDKG
19:9(10)	exaudi	gehyr V:	CBDKG
24:3(4)	vias	wegas V:	CBDKG
24:4(5)	dirige	gerece V:	CBDKG
24:5(6)	reminiscere	wes þu gemyndig V:	gemyne CBDG gemildsunga K
24:6(7)	ne memineris	ne gemynega V:	ne geman þu C, no þu gemyne B, ne gemun þu D and so KG

24:6(7)	magnam misericordiam (Ga. secundum etc.)	m̲yclan m̲ildheortnysse	V: miclan etc. CBD neh þinre etc. K æfter etc. G
24:6(7)	memor esto	weorð ge̲myndig	V: gemyndig beo CBD gemyn min K and so G
27:10(10)	salvam fac populum tuum	hal do þin folc	V: CBDKG
27:10(10)	hereditate	ðin y̲rfe	V: yrfeweardnysse C and so BDKG
27:10(10)	rege	r̲ece	V: CBDKG
34:1(1)	iudica	d̲em	V: CBDKG
34:2(2)	adprehende	ge̲grip	V: CBDK, lac G
34:2(2)	in adiutorem	on f̲ultume	V: CBDK, lac G
34:3(3)	persecuntur	e̲htend syndon	V: iehtað C and so BDKG
40:4(5)	sana	h̲æl	V: D, gehæl CBK, lac G
43:27(26)	exsurge	a̲ris	V: CBDKG
50:10(11)	faciem	a̲nsyne	V: CBDKG
50:11(12)	cor mundum	h̲eortan clæne	V: CBDKG
50:11(12)	spiritum rectum	rihtne g̲ast	V: gast rihtne CBDG lac K
50:12(13)	proicias	aw̲yrp	V: awerp CB, awyrp/ascyhh DG lac K
50:13(14)	principali	e̲aldorlice	V: aldorlice CB, aldorlicum DG, lac K
51:6(9)	in vanitate	on i̲del gylp	V: on idylny̲sse C and so BDG, lac K

51:8(11)	confitebor	andette V: CB and so DG, lac K	
51:8(11)	in seculum	on þære worulde V: on worulde CBG aworld D, lac K	
52:1(2)	abhomina-biles	onsceoniendlice syndon V: onscuniyndlice C and so BD, ascunigend G, lac K	
52:3(3)	intellegens	andgyt V: ongytynde C and so BDG, lac K	
52:5(6)	trepida-verunt	forhtigað V: forhtodon C and so BDG, lac K	
52:7(7)	dabit	syleð V: sylyð C, seleð B, selð D, syllyð G, lac K	
52:7(7)	salutare	hælu V: hæle C and so BDG, lac K	
52:7(7)	captivitatem	hæftnyde V: hæftnyd C and so BDG, lac K	
53:3(5)	conspectum	*gesyhðe V: CBDKG	
53:3(5)	alieni	fremde V: BDKG: fremdan C	
53:4(6)	susceptor	andfengea V: andfenge C and so BDKG	
53:5(7)	veritate	soðfæst V: soðfæstnesse C and so BDKGA	
54:1(2)	exaudi	gehyr V: CDKG, geher B	
54:1(2)	dispexeris	forseoh V: CDK, forseh B, forseah G	
54:1(3)	intende	beheald V: CBDKG	
54:3(4)	molesti erant	wurdon..yfele and hefige V: hefiges wæron CB, hefigmode hy wæron D and so KG	
54:4(5)	formido mortis	fyrhtu deaðes V: fyrto deaðys C and so BDGK	
54:7(8)	elongavi	feor gewite V: feorude fleogynde C, afeorrode BDKG	

54:7(8)	mansi	wunode V: CBDKG
54:7(8)	solitudine	westene V: CBDKG
54:7(9)	expectabam	bide V: gebad C and so B, anbided D and so KG
54:8(10)	divide	todælan V: todæl CBDKG
54:8(10)	contradictionem	wiðercwyda V: wiðcwedenisse CBA, wiðercwedulnisse D and so KG
54:10(13)	supportassem (Ga. sustinuissem)	abere V: BG, forbære D and so CK
54:12(14)	dux	latteow V: BG, ladþeow C and so D, lædere K
54:12(14)	notus	æghwæs cuð V: cuða CB and so DKG
54:13(16)	in infernum viventes	on helle heonan lifigende V: on helle lifgynde C and so BDKG
54:15(17)	clamavi	cleopode V: C and so BDG, clypige K
54:19(20)	contaminaverunt	besmitað V: besmiton CBDKG
54:19(29)	commutatio	onwendednes V: B and so CDKG
54:21(22)	enutriet	fedeð V: afedyð C and so BDKG
54:22(23)	fluctuationem	yþende mod V: yðgunge C and so BDK, yþunga G
55:1(2)	misere	miltsa V: CBDKG
55:1(2)	homo	man V: CBKG, ungl D
55:6(7)	abscondent	gehyden V: ahydyð C and so B, behydaþ DKG
55:6(8)	nihilo	nowiht V: nohte CB, nahte DKG
55:7(9)	posui (Ga. posuisti)	sette V: gesette CB, asette D, asetest G, settest K

55:7(9)	in promisione	on g̲ehate V: CBG, on behate D, on behæsc K	
55:7(9)	conspectu	ges̲yhðe V: CBDG, ansyne K	
56:1(2)	miserere	mi̲ltsa V: CBDKG	
56:2(3)	qui benefe- cit mihi	ðe me we̲l dyde V: se þe wel gedyde mec C and so BDKG	
56:4(4)	veritatem	so̲ðfæst V: soðfæstnysse CBDK, soðfæst(..) G	
56:6(6)	exaltare	ah̲efe V: hefe upp C, uphefe BK, upahefe D, upahafen G	
56:7(7)	paraverunt	g̲earwodon V: gegearwudon C and so BDKG	
56:8(7)	foderunt	d̲ulfon V CBDG, dulfa K	
56:9(8)	paratum	g̲earo V: CBDKG	
56:11(10)	confitebor	a̲ndete V: andytte C and so BDKG	
56:12(11)	magnificata	m̲ycel V: gemiclod C and so BDKG	
56:12(11)	misericordia	mi̲ldheortnes V: CBDKG	
57:1(2)	loquimini	so̲ð s̲precan V: sprecað CBDG, specan K	
57:1(2)	iudicate	demað̲ V: CBDKG	
57:3(4)	alienati sunt	f̲remde wurdon V: afremdode B, fremedlætede D, fremede K, fremedlæcede G	
57:4(6)	incantantium	he̲ahgaldor V: galyndra C and so B, ongalendra D and so KG	
57:7(9)	cera	we̲ax V: BDKG, wex C	
57:7(9)	viderunt	ges̲eoð V: gesawon CBDG, gesegan K	
57:9(11)	impiorum	a̲rleasan V: arleasra CBD, not in K or G	

57:10(12)	fructus	wæstm V: CBDG, wæsm K
58:2(3)	eripe	genere V: CB, ungl D, nera KG
58:4(6)	vide	gesyhst V: geseoh CBDKG
58:5(6)	ad visitandas	wylle/geneosian V: geneosiynne C and so BDKG
58:5(6)	intende	beheald V: CBDKG
58:6(7)	famem	hungor V: hungyr C and so BDKG
58:10(12)	ostende	ætyw V: CBKG, oþeow D
58:12(13)	mendacio	on lige V: leasunge CBDG, mendatio K
58:13(14)	scient	witon V: CBDKG
58:13(14)	dominabitur	wealdeð V: wealdyð C and so BDKG
59:1(3)	iratus es	yrre wurde V: eorre ðu eart CBD and so KG
59:5(7)	dextra	≠swyðre hand V: swiðran CB and so DKG
59:5(8)	in sancto	on..halignesse V: halgan hys C, halgan BK, halgum DG
59:6(9)	galaad	Galaad V: CBADKG (either written in or left unglossed as for a proper name)
59:7(10)	calciamentum	gescy V: CBDKG
59:8(11)	deducet	gelædeð V: CBDKG
59:9(12)	virtutibus	mægene V: mægnum CB and so DG, strengðe K
59:11(13)	facimus virtutibus	us sceal mægenes gemet V: don we mægen CBDK, mægen/miht G
60:1(2)	a finibus	utgemærum V: from gemærum CBDKG
60:1(2)	in petra	on halne stan V: on stane CBDKG

60:1(2)	exaltasti	ahefe V: uppahofe C and so BK, upahefdest DG	
60:3(5)	inhabitabo	eardige V: ineardige C, eardige BDKG	
60:4(6)	hereditatem	yrfe V: yrfewerdnysse C and so BDK yrfewerd G	
60:5(8)	permanebit (Ga. permanet)	wunian ece V: þurhwunað CBDKG	
60:6(8)	requiret	seceð V: secyð C and so BDK, lac G	
61:2(3)	salutaris	ƒhælend V: halwenda CB, hælo DKG	
61:4(5)	maledicebant	wyrgedan V: wyrigdon C and so BD, ungl K, wyrg(...) G	
61:5(6)	patientia	geðylde V: geþyld CBDKG	
61:7(8)	spes	hyht V: CBDKG	
61:11(11)	divitiae	wealan V: welan CBDKG	
62:3(3)	deserto	westene V: westynne C and so BDKG	
62:8(9)	dextera	swiðre V: CBDKG	
62:9(10)	quæsierunt	sohton V: CBDKG	
62:9(11)	tradentur	wæron geseald V: syn seald C and so BDKG	
64:4(5)	beatus	eadig V: CBDKG	
64:5(5)	replebimur	fyllað V: beoð gefyllyde C and so BDKG	
64:6(6)	spes	hyht V: CBDKG	
64:6(6)	in mare longe	feor on sæ V: on sæ feorr C and so BDKG	
64:7(8)	conturbas	gedrefest V: CBDKG	
64:7(8)	fluctuam	yða V: CBDKG	

64:8(9)	habitant	eard nymað V: eardiað CBD, ungl k, ear(..) G
64:9(9)	vespere	æfentid V: æfynne CBDG, ungl K
64:10(10)	parasti (Ga. preparasti)	gegearwadest V: gegearwudest C and so BDKG
64:11(11)	multiplica generationes	mænige on moldan manna cynnes/on cneorisse V: gemonigfealdynd cneorisse C and so BDK, manigfyldigende gedropunga G
64:11(11)	stillicidiis	þurh dropunge V: dropunge CBDKG
64:12(12)	campi	feldas V: CBDKG
64:12(12)	replebuntur	beoð fylde V: CBDKG
64:14(13)	ovium	eowdesceapum V: sceapa CBDKG, scepa A
64:14(13)	clamabunt	cleopiað V: CBA and so D, clypedon K, clyp(..) G
65:1(2)	gloriam laudi	wuldres lof V: wuldur lofys C and so BDKG
65:2(3)	virtutis	mægenes V: mægnys C and so BDKG
65:4(5)	venite et videte	cumað nu and geseoð V: CBDKG
65:5(6)	aridam	drige V: CBDKG
65:8(9)	posuit	sette V: gesette C and so BDKG
65:10(11)	laquem	gryne V: CBDKG
66:1(2)	vultum	andwlitan V: CBDG, ansyne K
66:2(3)	viam	wegas V: weg CBDKG
66:4(5)	exultent	hæbbe gefean V: gefeon CB, gefægnian DKG
67:1(2)	fugiant	ɫfleoð V: fleon CBDKG

67:4(5)	iter facite	doð si̲ðfæt V: siðfæt doð CBDG, siðfæt K	
67:5(5)	facie	a̲nsyne V: CBDKG	
67:5(6)	patris or- fanorum	s̲teopcildum fæderas V: fædrys steop- cildra C and so BDKG	
67:10(10)	pluviam vol- untariam	w̲ilsumne regn V: ren wilsumne CBDKG	
67:12(12)	verbum evan- gelizantibus	word g̲odspellendum V: CBDG, word cyþendum K	
67:13(14)	dormiatis	s̲læpað V: s̲lapað CBDKG	
67:13(14)	deargentate	f̲ægeres seolfres V: besylfryde CBG, ofersylfrede D, of sylfrenean K	
67:16(17)	in finem	wið e̲nde V: in ende B, on ende CDKG	
67:20(20)	prosperum	ges̲unde V: CBDKG	
67:24(17)	ecclesiis	c̲iricean V: CBDKG	
67:26(27)	confirma	get̲ryme V: CDKG, lac B	
68:3(4)	fauces	g̲oman V: CDKG, lac B	
68:5(5)	rapui	r̲eafude V: CDKG, lac B	
68:6(6)	insipientam	þæt ic eom unw̲is V: unwisdom CDKG, lac B	
68:7(7)	erubescant	habban/s̲ceame V: scomiyn C, asca- migen DG and so K, lac B	
68:9(10)	comedit	æ̲t ormæte V: ytð C and so BDKG	
68:10(11)	ieiunio	f̲asten V: fæstynne CB and so DK, f(...)tene G	
68:15(16)	obsorbeat	fors̲welge V: CBDKG	
68:17(18)	avertas	ac̲yr V: acyrr C and so BDK, cyrre G

68:17(18)	puero	c̲nihte V: CBDK, cnihte/cilde G
68:20(21)	miseriam	y̲rmðu V: yrmþe C and so BDKG
68:20(21)	consolentem (Ga. consolaretur)	f̲refrend V: frefriynde C and so BDK frefrode G
68:21(22)	escam	m̲ete V: CBDKG
68:21(22)	potaverunt	d̲renctan V: CBDKG
68:22(23)	retribu- tionem	e̲dlean V: CBDKG
68:22(23)	scandalum	æwisce V: CBDKG
68:23(24)	incurva	a̲beged V: gebigyð C and so BDK, ongebigeð G
68:24(25)	effunde	ag̲eot V: CBDKG
68:24(25)	adprehendat (Ga. conp̲rehendat)	forg̲ripe V: gegripyð CBDG, fornime K
68:25(26)	inhabitet	sy one̲ardiendes V: oneardige CBDKG
68:26(27)	persecuti sunt	e̲htan ongunnon V: iehtynde synt C, oehtende wæron B, ehton DG, slagene synd K
68:26(27)	dolorem vulneram	w̲unda sar V: sar wunda CBDKG
68:26(27)	addiderunt	w̲ean ecton V: geictun C, to ecton B, geyhton DK, toehton G
68:28(29)	deleantur	syn ad̲ilgad V: syn adilgude CBDKG
68:28(29)	libro viven- tium	l̲ifigendra bocum V: bec libbyndra C and so BDKG
68:28(29)	scribantur	wesen aw̲ritene V: beoð etc. CB, synd etc. DKG
68:28(29)	pauper et dolens	s̲arig þearfa V: þearfa 7 sarig CBDG, færfa 7 fanc K

87

68:29(30)	vultus	andwlita V: CBD, not in K or G	
68:29(30)	suscepit	onfeng V: CB, afeng DK, lac G	
68:32(33)	videant	geseoð V: geseon CBDKG	
68:32(33)	quærite	seceað V: secað CBDKG	
68:33(34)	non sprevit (Ga. non despexit)	ɫna forhycgan V: ne forgohode CBDG ne forseh K	
68:36(36)	hereditate	yrfestol: yrfeweardnysse C and so BDKG	
69:6(6)	pauper	worldþearfa V þearfa CBDKG	
69:6(6)	egenus	wædla V: CBDKG	
69:7(6)	liberator	alysend V: alysynd C and so BDKG	
69:7(6)	tardaveris (Ga. moreris)	lata þu V: CBDKG	
70:2(2)	inclina	ahyld V: C, onheld BDKG	
70:2(3)	munitum	trume V: getrymde C and so BDKG	
70:4(5)	iuventi	geoguðe V: iuguðe CD, gigoðhade B, geohgeþe K, geoguðes G	
70:8(9)	proicias	aweorp V: B, awerp C, awyrp DK, aw(...) G	
70:8(9)	derelinquas	forlæt V: CBDKG	
70:10(11)	dicentes	cweþað V: cweðende CBDKG	
70:10(11)	conprehendite	forgripen V: gegripað CBDKG	
70:12(13)	pudore	sceamu V: sceame CBDKG	
70:16(17)	iuventute	geoguðhade V: iuguðe C and so BDKG	
70:20(22)	confitebor	andette V: andytte C and so BDKG	
70:20(22)	vasis	sealmfatum V: fatum CBDKG	

70:21(23)	cantavero	s̱inge V: CBDKG
84:4(5)	deus salutaris noster	hælend drihten V: god halwenda ure CB / god hǣlo ure DG and so K
87:13(14)	mane	m̱orgena V: on morgynne C and so BDG, merien K
89:19(17)	splendor	ḇeorhtnys V: CBDKG
89:19(17)	opus manuum	ḫandgeweorc V: worc handa CBDKG
94:2(2)	faciem	a̱nsyne V: onsyne C and so BDKG
94:2(2)	confessione	a̱ndettan V: andytnysse C and so BDKG
94:6(6)	fecit	w̱orhte V: geworhte CB and so DKG
94:9(9)	viderunt	ges̱awon V CBDG, gesegan K
102:1(1)	benedic	ḇletsa V: CBDKG
102:1(1)	omnia interiora (Ga. omnia intra me sunt)	e̱all min ḭnneran V: ealle þa innyran CBD, ealle þa oninna me synd K, þe wiðinnan G
102:2(2)	noli oblivisci	ne wilt o̱fergeottul V: nelle þu ofyrgytan CBDKG
102:3(3)	languores (Ga. infirmitates)	a̱dle V: adla CBD, untruman K, untrumnesse G
102:4(4)	interitu vitam	ḻif ḻeof of forwyrde V: of forwyrde lif CBDKG
118:175	vivet	ḻeofað V: lyfað C and so BKG, lifige D
118:175	laudabit	ḻustum hereð V: heryð C and so BDG, hera K
118:175	iudica	ḏomas V: CBDKG
118:176	erravi	geḏwelede V: dwelude C and so BDKG
118:176	ovis	ḏysige sceap V: scep CBDKG
118:176	perierat	forw̱urðan w̱olde V: forwearð CBDKG

89

118:176	mandata	beboda V: bebodu CBD and so KG	
133:2(1)	atriis	cæfertunum V: cafyrtunum C and so BD, cavertune K, fafertunum G	
133:3(2)	noctibus	nihta V: nihtum CDKG, nihtibus B	
139:1(2)	eripe	genere V: CBDKG	
139:1(2)	ab homo malo fram yfelum men V: B, fram men yfelum CD and so KG		
140:2(2)	dirigatur	sy gereht V: syn gereht CD, lac B, ge(...)ehte K, (..)reht G	
148:1(1)	laudate	heriað V: hergeað CDKG, lacuna B pass. 148-150.	
148:2(2)	virtutes	leodmægen V: mægynu C, mægen DKG	
148:5(5)	facta sunt	wæron geworht V: wordyne synd CDKG	
148:5(5)	creata sunt	gesceapene wærun V: gesceapyne synd CDKG	
148:10(10)	bestie et universa pecora	deor and neat V: wildeor 7 nytenu CDKG	
148:10(10)	serpentes	nædran cynn V: næddran CDKG	
148:10(10)	volucres pennate	fugla cynn fiðerum gescyrped V: fuglas gefyðryde CDKG	
148:11(11)	reges terre	eorðcyningas V: cyninga eorðan CDKG	
148:13(13)	exaltatum est	ofer ealle is/ahafen V: uppahafyn CDKG	
148:13(14)	confessio	andetness V: andytnys CDKG	
149:1(1)	cantate	singað V: CDKG	
149:4(4)	mansuetos	manþwærum V: manþwærer C, manþwæran DKG	
149:5(5)	letabuntur (Ga. exultabunt)	beoð bliðe gedreme V: blissiað CD, gefægniað/blissiað G, glædiaþ K	

149:7(7)	ad facien- dam vinctam	mid þy hi wrecam þenceað V:to doyenne wrace C, to donne wrace IKG
149:7(7)	increpa- tiones	ðrea V: þreaung CG, ðreanga DK

COMMENTARY ON COLLATION LIST 3X

24:5(6) reminiscere: wes þu gemyndig in V provides metrical syllabic requirements for the line. K varies from DG in reading gemildsunga.

24:6(7) ne memineris: the D family differs in form from the A family: note these slight differences throughout the entries listed here.

24:6(7) magnam misericordiam: K and G follow the Ga. text secundum etc. by neh þinre (K) and æfter (G).

27:10(10) hereditate: yrfe in V is shortened to fit the meter.

34:2(2) adprehende: also in adiutorem: the lacuna in G is due to fire damage on the edge of fol. 41v.

34:3(3) persecuntur: ehtend syndon in V is extended to fit the meter.

50:12(13) proicias: D and G show a double gloss of the A tradition and a different reading.

51:6(9) in vanitate: V extends the gloss to a phrase for metrical reasons and literary effect.

53:3(5) conspectum: K preserves a singular reading.

54:3(4) molesti erant: V extends the gloss to a phrase for metrical reasons and literary effect.

54:7(8) elongavi: note the reading fleogynde in C, suggesting interpretation rather than a literal translation.

54:8(10)	<u>contradictionem</u>: the D family differs in word form from the A family.
54:10(13)	<u>supportassem</u>: note the unusual alignment of BG and CDK. Neither Gallican psalter pays attention to the Ga. emendation, <u>sustinuissem</u>.
54:12(14)	<u>dux</u>: K preserves a singular reading.
54:12(14)	<u>notus</u>: V adds æghwæs to <u>cuð</u> for alliteration.
54:13(16)	in <u>infernum</u> <u>viventes</u>: V adds <u>heonan</u> for metrical and alliteration purposes.
54:22(23)	<u>fluctuationem</u>: V's <u>yðende</u> <u>mod</u> reflects the element of poetic paraphrase, rather than translation, at work.
55:1(2)	<u>homo</u>: if we may assume D to be an educational text, D's lack of gloss here, as elsewhere, suggests that the lemma was now familiar to the glossator and could be recognized on sight: hence no translation would be necessary.
55:6(7)	<u>abscondent</u>: the D family differs in its prefix from the A family.
55:7(9)	<u>posui</u>: D and G preserve an "a"-prefix, and K and G follow the Ga. text <u>posuisti</u> in verb form.
55:7(9)	in <u>promisione</u>: K preserves a singular reading.
55:7(9)	<u>conspectu</u>: K preserves a singular reading.
56:6(6)	<u>exaltare</u>: I have listed the various readings for the lemma in all five psalters as they relate to V.
57:1(2)	<u>loquimini</u>: V again shows poetic paraphrase tendencies here with <u>soð</u> <u>sprecan</u>, as well as providing for alliteration. K reads <u>specan</u>, which may be a scribal error, or perhaps another singular reading.
57:4(6)	<u>incantantium</u>: V adds "<u>heah</u>"to <u>galdor</u> for alliteration purposes. The D family preserves an "<u>on</u>"-prefix.

57:9(11)	*impiorum*: K and G follow the Ga. text.
57:10(12)	*fructus*: K reads *wæsm*, which is probably an error for *wæstm* elsewhere.
58:12(13)	*mendacio*: V alters word order for line stress: K preserves a Latinate reading.
59:5(7)	*dextra*: V amplifies the gloss by adding *hand* to *swyðre* for alliteration purposes.
59:5(8)	*in sancto*: V's translation *on..halignesse* is not strictly accurate, since *halignesse* has a different shade of meaning from *halgum* ("sanctity" as opposed to "sanctuary"): this again may be the result of creative paraphrase.
59:9(12)	*virtutibus*: K preserves a singular reading.
59:11(13)	*facimus virtutem*: *gemet* in V is added for scansion and alliteration. G double-glosses *virtutem* with the two commonest translations for it.
60:1(2)	*a finibus*: V adds *ut* for alliteration purposes.
60:1(2)	*in petra*: V adds *halne* for meter and alliteration.
60:4(6)	*hereditatem*: As in 27:9(10), V shortens the gloss reading to *yrfe* for metrical purposes.
60:5(8)	*permanebit*: V translates this lemma *wunian ece* instead of *þurhwunað* to intensify the effect of the line, as well as to fit the stress pattern and metrical requirements.
60:6(8)	*requiret*: the lacuna in G is due to marginal crumbling at fol. 62v.
64:11(11)	*multiplica generationes*: V amplifies the gloss for *multiplica* to provide a 3-alliterator stress "m" alliteration in the first line, and uses *cneorisse* for *generationes* to alliterate in the second line.
64:14(13)	*ovium*: V expands *sceapa* to *eowdesceapum* to provide a vowel alliteration.

65:4(5)	venite et videte: V adds nu for metrical and compositional purposes.
66:1(2)	vultum: K renders this lemma ansyne, a gloss usually used for faciem.
67:5(6)	patris orfanorum: V inverts word order for metrical purposes
67:10(10)	pluviam voluntariam: V inverts word order for metrical purposes.
67:10(10)	verbum evangelizantibus: K preserves a singular reading.
67:13(14)	deargentate: V adds the modifier fægeres to provide an "f" alliteration: G accords with CB, while D and K each differ slightly in prepositional prefixes.
68:6(6)	insipientam: V expands the lemma gloss unwisdom to a phrase.
68:7(7)	erubescant: V expands the gloss to a phrase.
68:9(10)	comedit: the ormæte which follow V's translation æt, may be a modifier for ellenwod of the previous line, or may be intended in an adverbial sense (emend thus to ormætlice, and translate "Therefore the mighty zeal of thy house hath greatly devoured me").
68:10(11)	ieiunio: the lacuna in G is due to marginal damage at fol. 68v.
68:17(15)	puero: G double-glosses this lemma with the common reading cnihte, and a plausible direct translation, cilde.
68:24(25)	adprehendat: G follows the Ro. text while K appears to follow the Ga. emendation conprehendat with fornime.
68:26(27)	dolorem vulneram: V inverts word order for metrical purposes.
68:28(29)	libro viventium: V inverts word order for metrical purposes.

68:28(29)	scribantur: V uses the auxiliary verb wesan, instead of beoð or synd, for alliteration.
68:29(30)	pauper et dolens: V inverts word order for metrical purposes. K's reading is the result of scribal error and, unemended, is unintelligible.
68:29(30)	vultus: K and G follow the Ga. text.
68:29(30)	suscepit: the lacuna in G is due to marginal crumbling at fol. 69v.
68:33(34)	non sprevit: K appears to follow the Ga. text non despexit with na forseh, while G follows the the Ro. text.
68:36(36)	hereditate: V renders the lemma as yrfestol ("inheritance seat"), for compositional purposes.
69:6(6)	pauper: V extends the gloss to worldþearfa for a "w" alliteration.
70:4(5)	iuventi: B's form gigoðhade differs in suffix from that of V, C, D, K, and G.
70:8(9)	proicias: the lacuna in G is due to marginal damage at fol. 70v.
70:10(11)	dicentes: V changes the verb form for compositional purposes.
70:20(22)	vasis: V expands the gloss to the hapax legomenon sealmfatum (functioning perhaps as a kenning?) to provide an "s" alliteration. The exact translation of this word into modern English has not yet been established.
84:4(5)	deus salutaris noster: V prefers drihten to god here for deus, for metrical reasons.
87:13(14)	mane: K preserves a singular reading.
89:19(17)	splendor: read beorhtnes in Krapp, p.61.
89:19(17)	opus manuum: V joins the lemma words into a compound for alliteration.

94:2(2)	confessione: V changes its translation from noun to verb for compositional purposes.
94:9(9)	viderunt: gesegan in K is an Anglian form.
102:1(1)	omnia interiora: K and G follow the Ga. text omnia quæ intra me sunt.
102:2(2)	noli oblivisci: read ofergeottul in Krapp, p.74.
102:3(3)	languores: K and G follow the Ga. text infirmitates with untruman etc.
102:4(4)	interitu vitam: V adds the modifier leof for alliteration purposes.
118:175	laudabit: V adds lustum to the lemma gloss hereð for alliteration purposes.
118:176	ovis: V adds the modifier dysige for alliteration purposes. Read scep in Krapp, p.118.
118:176	perierat: read forweorðan wolde in Krapp, p.118.
133:2(1)	atriis: fafertunum in G is clearly the result of scribal error.
139:1(2)	ab homo malo: read menn in Krapp, p.136.
148:2(2)	virtutes: V expands the lemma gloss to read leodmægen ("nation-strength") to provide for an "l" alliteration.
148:10(10)	serpentes...volucres: V adds cynn to nædran and fugla for metrical and compositional purposes.
148:13(13)	exaltatum est: V expands its translation from the gloss to a phrase to provide alliteration and adequate syllables for meter.
149:5(5)	letabuntur: V, C and D accord on the Ro. text while B shows a lacuna. K follows the Ga. text with glædiaþ for exultabunt. However, although G double-glosses the lemma, it preserves the Ro. text gloss reading blissiað, and another gloss which does not accord with K.

149:7(7)   ad faciendam vinctam: V replaces the gloss
           doyenne/donne for faciendam, with þenceað for
           compositional purposes.

COLLATION LIST 3Y

5:1(2)	percipe	onfoh V: CBDG, opena K
5:2(4)	orabo	gebidde V: CBDKG
5:2(4)	exaudies	gehyr V: gehyrst C and so BDGK
5:3(5)	mane	on morgen V: CDK, on marne B, lac G
5:3(5)	adstabo	æt stande V: CBD, ungl K, lac G
19:9(10)	invocaverimus	cigen V: gecigað C and so BDKG
24:4(5)	doce	gelær V: lær CBDKG
27:10(10)	extolle	ahefe V: uppahefe C, uphefe BDKG
34:3(3)	conclude	beluc V: CBDKG
50:11(12)	innova	geniwa V: CBDG lac K
50:13(14)	letitiam	blisse V: CBDG lac K
50:13(14)	confirma	getryme V: CBDG lac K
51:8(11)	conspectum	gesyhðe V: CBDG lac K
52:1(1)	dixit	cwæð V: CG, ungl B, cwæ(..)ð D, lac K
52:3(3)	requirans	secan V: secynde C and so BDG, lac K
52:5(6)	timore	egesan V: ege C, for ege B, of ege DG, lac K
52:5(6)	invocaverunt	ciegan V: gecigdon CDG, gecedun A, gecedom B, lac K

52:8(7)	letabitur	byð..bliðe V: geblissod C and so BDG, <u>lac</u> K
53:1(3)	fac	gedo V: do CBDKG
53:1(3)	virtute	mægen V: mægyne C and so BDG, mihte K
53:2(4)	percipe	onfoh V: C and so BDKG
53:3(5)	proposuerunt	setton V: foresetton CBDKG
53:6(8)	confitebor	andette V: andytte C and so BDKG
54:1(2)	deprecationem	bene V: CBDKG
54:4(5)	conturbatum	gedrefed V: CBDKG
54:5(6)	venerunt	forcwomon V: cwoman CB, <u>ungl</u> D, com KG
54:6(7)	dabit	sealde V: sylyð C and so BDG, gyfð K
54:19(20)	timuerunt	ondrædað V: ondredon C and so BDKG
54:19(22)	divisi sunt	adælde V: todælde synd C and so BDKG
54:19(22)	adpropiabit	wæs neah V: toneahlæhte c and so BDKG
55:2(3)	conculaverunt	tredað V: fortrædon CBDKG
55:4(5)	laudabo	herige V: herge CB and so DKG
55:5(6)	verba	word V: CBDKG
56:1(2)	confidet	getryweð V: getrywyð C and so BDG, hihtað K
56:2(3)	clamabo	cleopige V: clypige C and so BDKG
56:3(4)	misit	onsende V: sende CBDKG
56:7(7)	laqueos (Ga. laqueum)	grine V: CBDKG

56:7(7)	incurvaverunt	onbigdon V: gebegdon CB and so DKG
56:8(7)	foveam	seað V: CBDG, pyt K
56:8(7)	inciderunt	gefeollan V: CBDG, infeollan K
56:10(9)	exsurge	aris V: CBDKG
56:11(10)	gentes (Ga. gentibus)	þeode V: þeoda CBDKG
57:1(2)	iuste (Ga. rectæ)	rihtum V: rihtan CG and so B, riht DK
57:4(5)	serpentis	nædran V: CBDKG
57:7(9)	liquefacta	melteð V: CBDK, not in G
57:8(10)	obsorbet	forswelgene V: forswelgyð C and so BDKG
57:9(11)	lavabit	ðwehð V: ðwyhð C and so BDG, wæxt K
57:10(12)	dicet	cweþeð V: cwið CB and so DKG
57:11(12)	iudicans	gedemeð V: demynde C and so BDKG
58:2(3)	operantibus	þe..wyrceað V: wyrcendum C and so BDG, wyrcende K
58:2(4)	salva	gehæle V: CB and so DKG
58:4(5)	cucurri	geanryne V: arn CBDK, ar(..) G
58:7(8)	loquentur	spræce V: sprecað CBG, lac D, specað K
58:7(8)	gladius	sweord V: swyrd C and so BKG, lac D
58:9(10)	custodiam	gehealde V: CG and so D, heale B, hælde K
58:9(10)	susceptor	andfencgea V: andfenge CG, ondfengea B, andfeng DK

58:12(13)	delicta (Ga. delictum)	scyld V: scylda CB and so DG, scyl K
59:1(3)	misertus	milde V: mildsiynd C and so BK, gemiltsod DG
59:3(5)	potasti	drenctest V: drenctes CBDKG
59:3(5)	ostendisti	ætywdest V: CBK, oðeowdes D, aþeowdest G
59:5(8)	locutus est	aspræce V: sprecende is CB and so DG, specende is K
59:5(8)	dividam (Ga. partibor)	gedæle V: todæle CDK, todælo B, ungl G
59:7(9)	Juda	Iuda V: ABCD, ungl G, christus K
59:7(10)	in idumea	Idumea V: CBDK, idumealande G
59:7(10)	extendam	aðenige V: CBDK, aþenne G
59:8(11)	civitatem	ceastre V: cestre C and so BDKG
59:9(12)	egredieris	ga V: gæst CBG, utgæst DK
59:10(13)	auxilium	fultum V: CBDKG
59:10(13)	vana	idel V: CBDKG
60:1(2)	oratione	gebed V: CBDKG
61:1(2)	subdita est	wylle..underþeodan V: undyrþeodyð and so B, underþeod bið DKG
61:4(5)	cogitaverunt	þohton V: CBDKG
61:5(6)	verumptamen	hwæðere V: CBDG, þeh hwæþere K
61:11(11)	affluant	flowen V: toflowyn C and so B, ætflowan DK, æt(..) G
62:1(2)	vigilo	wacie V: wacige C and so BDKG
62:2(2)	sitivit	þyrsteð V: þyrstyð CB, þyrste DKG

62:3(3)	apparui	ætywe V:	ætywde CK and so BG, oþeowde D
62:7(7)	memor fui	gemynd..begange V:	gemyndig wæs CBDKG
62:8(9)	suscepit	onfencg V:	onfeng CBDKG
62:10(12)	iurant	sweriað V:	CKG, swergeað BD
63:4(6)	firmaverunt	trymmað V:	trymydon C and so BDKG
63:7(8)	plage	hyra wita V:	wite C and so BDK, lac G
63:8(9)	conturbati	gedrefede V:	CBDKG
63:8(10)	timuit	sceal..ondrædan V:	dræt C, ondred B, adred DKG
63:8(10)	intellexerunt	ongitan V:	ongeton CB, angeaton D and so KG
64:5(5)	templum	templ V:	tempyl C and so BDKG
64:9(9)	exitus	gancg V:	utgang CBDG, ungl K
64:14(14)	frumento	hwætum V:	hwæte CBADKG
65:1(2)	date	syllað V:	CG, sellað BD, gifað K
65:6(7)	dominabitur	wealdeð V:	wealdyð C, waldeð B, wyldeþ DKG
65:10(11)	induxisti	gelæddest V:	ingelæddyst C, gelæddes B and so DG, alæddest K
65:12(13)	reddam	gylde V:	agylde C and so BDKG
65:12(14)	distinxerunt	gedældon V:	todældon CBDKG
65:17(19)	deprecationis	bene V:	CBDKG
66:1(2)	inluminet	leohte V:	onlyhte CBDKG

66:3(4)	confiteantur	andettan V: G, andyttyn C and so BDK
66:6(7)	fructum	wæstme V: CBDKG
67:5(5)	turbabuntur	wesan gedrefde V: beoð gedrefyde C and so BDKG
67:5(6)	iudicis	æt dome V: deman CBDKG
67:7(7)	educit	gelædeð V: utalædeð CB, alædeþ DKG
67:9(9)	distillaverunt	droppetað V: dropydon CB, drupon DG, dropan K
67:11(11)	pauperes	þearfum V: þearfan CBDKG
67:14(15)	discernit	toscadeð V: tosceadyð C and so BDKG
67:15(16)	uberem	genihte V: genihtsum C and so BD, not in K or G
67:18(19)	ascendens	astah V: stigynde CB, astigende DK, astige G
67:23(25)	visi sunt (Ga. viderunt)	wæron gesewene V: CBDK, gesawon G
67:24(26)	prævenerunt	coman V: forecwomun CBDKG
67:24(26)	iuvenum (Ga. iuvencularum)	geongra V: gingra CB, iungra D, gingrena G, glimæidina K
67:25(28)	adolescentior	on geoguðe V: iongysta C, geondra DK, lac B, (..)esta G
67:26(29)	manda	bebeod V: CDKG, lac B
67:27(31)	increpa	þreatast V: þrea CDKG, lac B
68:1(3)	substantia	sped V: CDKG, lac B
68:2(3)	demersit	besencte V: CDKG, lac B
68:3(4)	raucæ	hase V: CDKG, lac B

68:5(5)	confortati	gestrangad V: gestrongode C and so DKG, lac B
68:5(5)	persecuntur (Ga. persecuti)	ehton V: ehtað CDK, ehtigende G, lac B
68:7(7)	requirunt (Ga. querunt)	seceað V: secað CBDKG
68:20(21)	quesivi	sohte V: CBD, not in K or G
68:21(22)	fel	geallan V: CBDKG
68:21(22)	aceto	ecede V: ecyde C and so BDKG
68:30(30)	laudabo	herige V: herge C and so BDK, lac G
68:31(32)	vitulum	cealf V: CBDKG
68:35(36)	salvam fecit	hæleð V: hale gedo CBDKG
68:35(36)	ædificabuntur	beoð..getimbrade V: CBDKG
68:35(36)	inhabitabunt	eard nimað V: oneardiað CBDKG
68:36(37)	diligunt	lufiað V: CBDKG
69:5(5)	lætentur	habban..blisse V: blissigen CBDKG
69:5(5)	diligunt	lufigean V: lufiað CBDK, (..)fiað G
69:5(5)	dicant	cweðen V: BDKG, cweðeð C and so A
70:2(3)	salvum facias	hæle V: halne gedo CBDKG
70:3(3)	firmamentum	trymmend V: getrymydnys C and so BDKG
70:4(5)	patientia	geþyld V: CBDKG
70:7(8)	repleatur	sy..gefylled V: CBDKG
70:7(8)	cantare (Ga. cantarem)	singan..mærsian V: singan CBDKG

70:8(9)	senectutis	ylde tid V: tide ylde C and so BDKG	
70:9(10)	consilium	geþeaht V: geðieht C and so BDKG	
70:10(11)	dereliquat	læte V: forlet CBDKG	
70:10(11)	persequimini	ehtan V: iehtað C and so BDKG	
70:12(13)	detrahentes	tældun V: tælynde CBDKG	
70:16(16)	memorabor	geman V: beo gemyndgod CB, gemyndig beo DKG	
70:16(17)	docuisti	lærdest V: DKG, gelærdyst C, lærdes B	
70:17(18)	generatione	cneorisse V: CBDG, cyþnesse K	
70:19(20)	conversus	oncyrdest V: gecyrde C, gecerred BDKG	
70:21(23)	gaudebunt (Ga. exultebunt)	gefeoð V: CB, gefeogað D, gefeoð /blissiað G, blissiaþ K	
70:21(23)	redemisti	lysdest V: alysidyst C and so BDKG	
79:18(29)	ostende	æteow V: ætyw CG, (..)teaw B, oteaw A, oðeaw D, anyw K	
84:4(5)	averte	oncyrr V: acyrr CB and so KG, framacyrr D	
87:13(14)	clamavi	clypode V: clypige C, cleopode BDKG	
89:19(17)	dirige	gerece V: CBDK, gere(..) G	
94:8(8)	obdurare	forhyrden V: geheardian C, aheardian BG, wiðheardian DK	
94:11(11)	cognoverunt	oncneowan V: CBDKG	
101:1(2)	perveniet (Ga. veniet)	becume V: BD, becumað C, cume KG	
102:3(3)	sanat	gehælde V: gehælyð CBDKG	

118:175	anima	sawul V: sawl CBDKG	
118:176	require (Ga. quare)	sec V: C and so BDKG	
121:7(7)	habundantia	genihtsum V: genihtsumnys C and so BDKG	
121:7(7)	fiat pax	sy..sybb V: CBDG, gewyrpe sib K	
133:2(1)	statis	standað V: stondað CBDKG	
133:3(2)	extollite	hebbað V: uphebbað CB, ahebbað DKG	
148:6(6)	preceptum	bebod V: bybod C and so DKG, lac B	
148:12(12)	virgines	glade fæmnan V: fæmnan CDG, lac B, mæidena K	
149:2(2)	letentur	blissien V: blissie CDKG, lac B	
150:2(2)	tube	beman V: byman C and so DKG, lac B	

COMMENTARY FOR COLLATION LIST 3Y

5:1(2)   percipe: K preserves a singular reading.

5:3(5)   mane: B preserves an unusual variation of the gloss.

53:1(2) virtute: K preserves a singular reading.

53:3(5) proposuerunt: V prefers the simplex setton to the complex foresetton which accords with the lemma.

54:1(2) deprecationem: K preserves a singular reading.

54:6(7) dabit: K preserves a singular reading.

54:19(22) adpropiabit: V renders the lemma gloss as a modified phrase, wæs neah.

55:2(3)	conculaverunt: V reads tredað as opposed to the complex fortrædon.
56:1(2)	confidet: K preserves a singular reading.
56:8(7)	foveam: K preserves a singular reading.
56:8(7)	inciderunt: K adds the prefix "in"- to the lemma gloss.
57:7(9)	liquefacta: this lemma does not appear in G.
57:9(11)	lavabit: K preserves a singular reading.
58:7(8)	loquentur: as elsewhere, (cf. 59:5(8)), K prefers specan to spræcan.
59:7(9)	Juda: K preserves the singular, perhaps etymologically interpretive christus here.
51:11(11)	affluant: the partial lemma in G is due to fire damage at fol. 63r.
62:7(7)	memor fui: V renders fui as begange rather than wæs.
65:1(2)	date: K preserves a singular reading here as in 54:6(7).
67:15(16)	uberem: K and G follow the Ga. text.
67:23(25)	visi sunt: K follows the Ro. text while G follows the Ga. text.
67:24(26)	iuvenum: K preserves this unusual gloss, glimæidina, which also appears as a double gloss gliewmedene/plegiendra in E (Harsley, p.114).
67:25(28)	adolescentior: the partial lacuna in G is due to damage on the margin of fol. 67v.
68:5(5)	persecuntur: G follows the Ga. text with a participial form of the lemma gloss.
68:20(21)	quesivi: K and G follow the Ga. text.
68:30(30)	laudabo: the lacuna in G is due to marginal crumbling on fol. 69v.

68:35(36)	inhabitabunt: V renders this as eard nimað rather than oneardiað perhaps for compositional reasons. It belongs in a line with no apparent alliteration, but the expansion of the gloss may function metrically in some fashion.
70:8(9)	senectutis: V inverts word order perhaps for emphasis in the line.
70:21(23)	gaudebunt: K seems to follow the Ga. text exultebunt with blissiaþ, while G double-glosses the lemma with the Ro. and Ga. translations respectively.
84:4(5)	averte: D amplifies the gloss with the prefix "fram". Read oncyrre in Krapp, p.52.
87:13(14)	clamavi: read clypade in Krapp, p.55.
101:1(2)	perveniet: K and G follow the Ga. text veniet with cume.
118:175	anima: read sawl in Krapp, p.118.
118:176	require: read sece in Krapp, p.118.
121:7(7)	fiat pax: read si sib in Krapp, p.120.
148:12(12)	virgines: V adds the modifier glade to fæmnan for compositional purposes. K preserves the singular gloss mæidena here.

COLLATION LIST 3X1

53:1(3)	libera (Ga. iudica)	alys V: alies, B, lac K, alyse D gefreo C, gefrea A, dem G V APPEARS TO FOLLOW THE TRADITION OF THE D FAMILY
54:14(16)	hospitis (Ga. habitaculis)	gasthusum V: gysthusum C and so BK, A, D. eardunggum/on eardungstowe G V APPEARS TO FOLLOW A TRADITION COMMON TO BOTH THE A AND D FAMILY

54:17(19)	liberabit	a̲lyse V: aliesde B and so G, alyseþ D gefreoð C, gefreað A TRADITION: D
56:3(4)	liberavit	a̲lysde V: aliesde B and so KG, alysde D, gefreode C and so A. TRAD: D
56:4(5)	dormivi	wæs s̲læpende V: slep BKG, slep D hnappude C, hneappade A TRAD: D
56:5(5)	arma et sagittæ	w̲æpenstrælas V: wæpyn 7 strælas B and so G, A, D wæpyn 7 flana C and so K TRAD: A/D
58:1(2)	libera	a̲lys V: BKG, D gefreo C, gefrea A. TRAD: D
59:4(6)	liberentur	wæron a̲lysde V: sien aliesde B and so KG, D. gefreode C and so A TRAD: D
59:7(10)	olla spei	h̲yhtes h̲wer V: hihtys hwer CB(J), hwer hyhtes A, D crocca hiht K(FI) crocca hwer hihtes G TRAD: A/D
61:9(10)	stateris	on w̲ægum V: CBG, lac̲ K, A anmittum D. V APPEARS TO FOLLOW THE TRADI- TION OF THE A FAMILY
61:10(11)	rapinis	r̲eaflace V: reiflac C and so K, reaflacum D gestrodu B and so A, lac̲ G TRAD: D
64:4(5)	inhabitabit	e̲ardað V: ineardað CB, A, D, oneardaþ K gefylled G. TRAD: A/D

65:3(4)	dicat	secge V: C and so G, secge D singe K, cwið B and so A TRAD: D
67:4(5)	ascendite	astah V: astag BKG, A, D upastag C. TRAD: A/D
67:16(17)	suscipitis (Ga. suspicamini)	onfoð V: CK, A, D, lac B wene ge G. TRAD:A/D
67:21(22)	delictis	scyldum V: BKG, A, D gyltum C. TRAD:A/D
68:6(6)	scis	wast V: CK, A, D, lac B eart G. TRAD: A/D
68:18(19)	libera	ⱡalys V: BKG, D gefreo C, gefrea A. TRAD: D
68:24(25)	indignatio (Ga. furor ire)	æbylignes V: æbylh þu CB, ehbylgðu A, æbylgnis D wraðe yrre K, hat- heortnesse G TRAD: A/D
102:3(3)	propitiatur	miltsade V: milde bið B, gemiltsað G, milde A arfull/milde bið C arfæstað K, arfæst D TRAD: A
149:1(1)	canticum novum	ⱡneowne sang V: sang niwne CKG, song neowne A lac B, cantic niwne D TRAD: A
149:1(1)	ecclesia sanctorum	on haligra/clænre cyricean V: cyrcean haligra CG, cirican haligre A lac B, gesomnunga haligra DK TRAD: A

COLLATION LIST 3Y1

40:4(5)	dixi	cweðe V: BK, <u>lac</u> G, cweð A, D sæde C. TRAD: A/D
52:3(3)	dominus (Ga. deus)	drihten V: CB, <u>lac</u> K, dryhten A,D god G. TRAD: A/D
52:5(5)	operantur	wyrceað V: CB, <u>lac</u> K, wircað A, wyrcað D, cyrrað G. TRAD: A/D
52:8(7)	iacob	Iacob V: CBG, A, <u>lac</u> k se gecorena D: TRAD: A
54:10(13)	maledixisset	wyrgde V: wyrgde C, wyride K, wyrgde D wergcweodolode B, wegcweo- delade A, wyrig/cwedelode G TRAD: D
55:5(6)	consilia (Ga. cogitationes)	geðeaht V: CB, geðæht A, geþeaht D, geþances K, spræc G TRAD: A/D
55:6(7)	expectavit (Ga. sustinuerunt)	bad V: gebad CB, A, anbidode DK forþyldegodon G. TRAD:A/D
55:7(9)	nuntiavi	secge V: sægde C, secge B, segde A cyðde/ic secge G cyþde D, cyþe K, TRAD: A TRAD: A
65:2(3)	mentientur	leogað V: BKG, D, legað A leasiað C. TRAD: A/D
67:7(7)	provocant (Ga. exasperant)	beoð gecigde V: C, forðgecigað D and so K gremmað B and so A tyrwiað G. TRAD: D

67:17(18)	currus	cræta V: cræt CKG, cræt D scrid B and so A. TRAD: D
68:6(6)	delicta	scylde V: scylde A, scyldas DG, lac B gylta C, leastras K TRAD: A/D
68:22(23)	mensa	beod V: CBKG, A mese D. TRAD: A
133:1(1)	ecce	efne V: CKG, A, D sehðe B. TRAD: A/D
149:8(8)	vinculis (Ga. manicis)	bendas V: bendum CK, A, D, lac B handcopsum G: TRAD: A/D

COMMENTARY ON LIST 3X1

53:1(3)   libera: V agrees with BD while K shows a lacuna.
            C and A display accordance with gefreo, and G
            follows the Ga. text iudica with dem, glossed
            similarly in J and F. H is unglossed here.

54:14(16)   hospitis: V accords with ABCD on the Ro. text
            translation, K also follows the Ro. text. G
            double-glosses this lemma after the Ga. text
            habitaculis, H is unglossed, while J reads
            eardungstowe and F reads eardungstowum, accord-
            ing with the second element of G's double gloss.

54:17(19)   liberabit: V accords with the D-family, as does
            B, while C follows A with gefreoð. It would
            seem likely, in light of the consistence of the
            agreement between B and D for this lemma, that
            there was some common element between the two
            glosses, although this makes no provision for the
            B-gloss being copied directly from the A-gloss
            (according to Kuhn) or for the original of D being
            a mid-tenth-century educational text as I have
            suggested. This question of the relationship
            between B and D, which appear to have a common

place of origin, certainly bears more investigation.

56:3(4) liberavit: as above, V accords with BDKG, while C accords with A. Wildhagen has no note on this for C, but other than liberare and its forms rendered alys (7:1) and alysend (17:3), the reading gefreodyst at 21:5 seems to mark C's dependence on A for this lemma gloss throughout the Psalter.

56:4(5) dormivi: V follows the D group with B, while C and A both preserve the unusual gloss hnappude for this lemma.

56:5(5) arma et sagittæ: V runs the psalter-gloss wæpyn 7 stræalas of ABGD together for metrical purposes, while K and C preserve the gloss flana for sagittæ. This same gloss occurs in F.

58:1(2) libera: as before, V accords with BDKG while C accords with A.

59:4(6) liberentur: V accords with BDKG while C accords with C.

59:7(10) olla spei: although this is not metrical alliteration, it is included here since it seems to function as some form of alliteration when read aloud. Two traditions are represented here; the first, which renders olla as hwer, includes A, D and V, together with B, C and J. The other psalters H, K, F and I render olla as crocca, while G double-glosses it crocca hwer.

61:9(10) stateris: V accords with A, B and C, with F and G also showing the Vespasian tradition and K showing a lacuna. D reads anmittum, which is also preserved in J and H.

61:10(11) rapinis: V accords with the Regius tradition's reaflacum, present also in K and C. G shows a lacuna, while B reads gestrodu after A.

64:4(5) inhabitabit: V agrees with ineardað of ABCD and oneardiaþ of K. G's gefylled seems to look ahead to replebimur (cf. Rosier, p.149), since F, J and H agree with K, oneardað.

65:3(4)   dicat: V agrees with D, secge, and so with C and
           G. K reads singe, and B reads cwið after A.

67:4(5)   ascendite: V accords with A, B, D, the uncorrected
           E-gloss, F, I, J, K and G, while C reads upastah,
           noted by Wildhagen as a singular reading.

67:16(17) suscipitis: V agrees with A, C, D and K. B
           shows a lacuna here. G reads wene ge, which may
           follow the Ga. text suspicamini, since J reads
           (tohwi) wene ge, and F reads wene ge. H is
           unglossed.

67:21(22) delictis: V agrees with A, B, D, K, G, J and
           the corrections in E, while the C reading,
           gyltum, occurs elsewhere in F, I and the uncorr-
           ected gloss in E.

68:6(6)   scis: V's wast agrees with A, C, D, K, J and F
           while the G reading eart occurs elsewhere in H
           (cf. Rosier, p.160).

68:18(19) libera: V agrees with BDKG while C and A accord.

68:24(25) indignatio: V accords generally with the read-
           ings in ABCD while K and G follow the Ga. text
           furor ire. K provides a singular reading wraðe
           yrre, while G's hatheortnesse is extended to
           hatheortnes yrres in J, H, and F.

102:3(3)   propitiatur: V agrees with A, B and G. C
           preserves a double gloss which represents both
           the A tradition and a variation ("arfull") on
           the DK reading arfæst. J and F also read arfæst,
           and H is unglossed,

149:1(1)   canticum novum: V follows A, C, K and G, and B
           shows a lacuna. D preserves a Latinate reading
           cantic niwne, which also occurs in J. H is
           unglossed and F reads lofsang.

149:1(1)   ecclesia sanctorum: V renders ecclesia as cyricean
           in accordance with A, C and G. B shows a lacuna,
           and D and K gloss ecclesia as gesomnunga along
           with J. H shows a lacuna, and F reads cyrcan
           after A.

COMMENTARY ON COLLATION LIST 3Y1

40:4(5)   dixi: V follows the so-called "TRAD: A/D", in which the A and D readings agree. B and K accord with A and D, G shows a lacuna, and C preserves a singular reading, sæde, which also appears in J. Wildhagen (p.99), notes that the prose part of P, J, and erroneously, A, accord with this reading in C.

52:3(3)   dominus: V accords with ABCD, while G translates the Ga. text deus as god. K shows a lacuna, but other Gallican psalters H, J and F also read god.

52:5(5)   operantur: V agrees with A, B, C and D here. K shows a lacuna, and G reads cyrrað which Rosier cannot explain (p.127) other than to note that J reads yrraþ. However, H also reads cyrrað, while F agrees with the A/D group by glossing the lemma weorcað.

52:8(7)   iacob: V agrees with ABCG in showing this as a proper name. K shows a lacuna, and D reads se gecorena, preserved elsewhere only in F. H is unglossed and J agrees with the A-group.

54:10(13)   maledixisset: wyrgeð in V agrees with CDK, while A and B preserve the longer compound wergcwedolode, and G splits the compound into a double gloss, wyrig/cwedelode. H, J and F agree with D.

55:5(6)   consilia: V agrees with ABCD, while K follows the Ga. text cogitationes with geþances, and G reads spræca. Rosier suggests (p.133) that the G-glossator looked to sermones in v.5.

55:6(7)   expectavit: V agrees closely with ABC, and generally with DK, while G follows the Ga. text sustinuerunt with forþyldegodon which appears elsewhere in J, F and I. H is unglossed.

65:2(3)   mentientur: V agrees with A, B, D, F, G, H, J, and K while C reads leasiað, which Wildhagen notes as a singular reading.

114

67:7(7)	provocant:	V agrees with C, and thereby with DK. B and A accord together with gegremmað, and G preserves the singular reading tyrwiað, while J and F read æbilgað and H remains unglossed.
67:17(18)	currus:	V accords with C, D, K and G, while B and A agree with scrid.
68:6(6)	delicta:	V follows A, D, J. L and G here with scylde, while the corrected E-gloss reads gyltas/scyldes, the uncorrected E reads ægyltas, and F, I and C read gylta. K preserves the singular gloss leastras.
68:22(23)	mensa:	V follows A, B, C, K and G, while D reads mese. F follows D with myse, and J reads beoþ/misa, while H is unglossed.
133:1(1)	ecce:	V agrees with A, C, D, K and G while B preserves sehðe as a singular reading.
149:8(8)	vinculis:	V accords with A, C, D and K, while B shows a lacuna. G renders the lemma as hand-copsum after the Ga. text manicis, as do F and J. H shows a lacuna.

COLLATION LIST 4X

5:1(2)	domine	wuldres ealdor V: drihtyn C and so BDKG
24:3(4)	notas (Ga. demonstra)	ǂwise V: cuðe CBD, cuðe gedo G, ætyw K
24:4(4)	veritate	ræde V: soðfæstnesse CBDKG
24:6(7)	iuventutis	þe is geong dyde: iuguþe C and so BK iuguðhades DG
32:18(22)	speravimus	wenað V: gehyhtað C and so BK hihton DG

34:2(2)	arma et scutum	gar and scyld	V: wæpn 7 scyld CBDK (..) 7 scyld G
34:3(3)	effunde	heald	V: ageot CBDK, lac G
34:3(3)	frameam	herewæpnum	V: swurd C and so B, flane DKG
40:4(5)	peccavi	firene fremede	V: syngode CBDKG
50:10(10)	peccatis	fræcnum fyrenum	V: synnum CBDG, lac K
50:11(11)	visceribus	gehigde	V: innoðum CBDG, lac K
51:7(10)	speravi	wat	V: gehihte CBDG, lac K
51:7(10)	olivia	elebeam	V: eletreow CB, eleberige DG, lac K
51:7(10)	in æternum	to worulde	V: on ecnesse CBDG, lac K
51:7(10)	misericordia	milde mod	V: mildheortnesse CBDG, lac K
52:1(1)	insipiens	unhydig	V: unwise CDG, ungl B lac K
52:2(2)	non est qui faciat bonum	næs þa goddænd	V: nys þe doo god C and so BDG, lac K
52:4(4)	declinaverunt	besegen	V: ahyldon C and so BDG, lac K
52:5(5)	iniquitatem	unrihtes	V: unrihtwisnesse CBDG (et passim), lac K
52:5(5)	cognoscent (Ga. sciant)	andgyt habban	V: oncnæwað CBD, hi ne witan G, lac K
52:5(5)	devorant	fretað	V: forswelgað CB, swelgað DG, lac K

52:6(6)	confusi sunt	beoð geh_yrwede V: gedrefyde CB, scynde hy synd DG, l_ac K
53:2(4)	verba oris mei	_agen word V: word muðes mines CBDKG
53:5(7)	averte	af_yr V: acyrr CBDKG
53:6(8)	voluntarie	_lustum _lace V: wi_llynlice C, wilsumlice BDG, willodlice K
53:7(9)	tribulatione	_earfoðum V: geswencednysse C, geswince BDKG
53:7(9)	eripuisti	_alysdest V: generedest C and so BDK, genered (..) G
54:2(3)	contristatus	grimme V: geunrotsod CBDKG
54:2(3)	conturbatus	_forhtige V: gedrefyd C and so BDKG
54:2(4)	tribulatione peccatoris	_fyrenfulra _fæcne niðas V: geswince synfullys C and so BDKG
54:7(9)	salvum facent	_bete V: halne gedyde C and so BDKG
54:10(12)	dolus	_man inwides V: facn CBDKG
54:12(15)	ambulavinus	_gangan V: eodon CBDKG
54:12(15)	consensu	ge_þeahtunge V: geþafunge CB, sybbe DK, gesibbe/mid geþafunge G
54:18(29)	humiliabit	geh_yreð V: geaðmodað C and so BDKG
54:19(21)	testamentum	gew_itnesse V: cyðnysse CBDKG
54:21(23)	iacta	_sete V: aworp C and so BDKG
54:23(24)	viri sanguinem	_blodhreowa wer V: weras blode CBDKG

54:23(24)	dolosi	b̲ealuinwites V: fæcnan CB, fæcenfulle DKG
54:23(24)	dimidiabunt	lif/gem̲eteð V: gemidliað CB, healfgetillað D and so K, getillað G
55:2(4)	ab altitudine diei	fram æ̲rmergene V: heanysse dægys C and so BDG, from heah- nes(..) K
55:3(4)	sperabo	w̲ene V: gehihte CBDKG
55:5(6)	execrabantur	s̲ocon V: onscunedon CBDKG
55:6(7)	calcaneum	h̲ælun V: hellspuran CB, hoh DK, hoh hellspuran G
55:8(10)	retrorsum	h̲inderling V: K, on bæc CB, underbecling DG
55:8(10)	agnovi (Ga. cognovi)	w̲at and can V: oncneow CBDG, gecneow K
55:10(12)	eripuisti	wiðl̲æddest V: generedyst C and so BDKG
55:10(13)	a lapsu (Ga. de lapsu)	f̲æle beweredest V: from slide CBDG, of slide K
56:1(2)	spero	gew̲icie V: gehihte CBDKG
56:2(3)	deum altissimum	h̲eahgode V: gode þan hehstan C and so BDKG
56:4(4)	misericordiam	m̲ilde gehigd V: mildheortnysse CBDKG
56:9(8)	dicam	s̲prece V: cweðe CBK, secge DG
56:10(9)	psalterium	w̲ynpsalterium V: hearpe CB, sealmleod DG, sealmleof K
57:2(3)	operamini	h̲ogedon V: wyrceað C and so BDKG

57:3(4)	peccatores	f̲irenfulle V: synfullan CBDKG
57:3(4)	erraverunt	l̲ygeword spæcon V: dwoledon B and so DKG, hleodrodon C
57:4(5)	aspidis	a̲spide V: nædran CBDKG
57:4(6)	incantantur (Ga. incantantis)	s̲ingað V: agalynde C, beoð agalene B, beoð begalene DG, ongalendra K
57:6(8)	deveniet	forw̲eorðan V: becumað CBDKG
57:6(8)	intendit	b̲endeð V: behealdyð C, aðeneð B, behylt DG, gebyið K
57:6(8)	infirmetur	a̲dl on seteð V: syn geuntrumude C and so BDKG
57:9(11)	iustus	soðf̲æst V: rihtwisa C and so BDKG
57:9(11)	peccatorum (Ga. peccatoris)	f̲yrenf̲ulra V: synfullys CBDK, synfullan G
58:1(2)	eripe	a̲hrede V: genere CB, (..)nere D, nera K
58:1(2)	insurgentibus	ðe me f̲eohtað V: arisyndum C and so BDKG
58:2(3)	iniquitatem	n̲ahtfremmendra V: unrihtwisnysse CBDKG
58:2(3)	viris sanguinem	blodhreowes weres V: weras blode C and so BDKG
58:3(4)	inruerunt	s̲tundum ongunnon V: onræsdon CB, onhruron D and so KG
58:10(12)	occideris	d̲o...to d̲eadan V: sleh C and so BDKG
58:10(12)	obliviscantur	a̲nforlæton V: ofyrgytyn C and so BDKG

58:11(12)	protector	w̱ealdend V:	gescyldynd CB, styhtend DG, frofer K
58:12(13)	conpellantur	ḻange feredon V:	sien genidde CB, syn anydde D, not in K or G
58:13(14)	iacob	m̱anna cynnes V:	Iacob CBDKG
58:16(17)	virtutem (Ga. fortitudinem)	s̱trengþu V:	strengðe K, mægyn C and so BDG
58:17(17)	refugium	ic ḫelpe æt ðe hæfde V:	gebeorg C̄B, frofer DKG
59:2(4)	mota est (Ga. commota est)	heo ahrered is V:	styryd heo ys C and so B, astyred DKG
59:3(4)	vino compunctionis	mid w̱ynsume w̱ine V:	mid wine on- bryrdnysse C and so BDKG
59:4(5)	metuentibus	þam þe ege ðinne ẹlne V:	ondræ- dyndum C and so BDKG
59:4(5)	significationem	ḇecnunge V:	getacnunge CB and so DG, tacuga K
59:4(5)	electi (Ga. dilecti)	ḻeofe þine V:	gecorynan C and so BDKG
59:4(6)	a facie arcus	ḇogan 7 stræle V:	from ansyne bogan C and so BDG, ungl K
59:8(11)	munitam	w̱eallum bew̱orhte V:	getrymede CB, gestrangode DK, ungl G
59:10(13)	tribulatione	on ẹarfoðum V:	geswencednysse C, geswince BKG, swencende/þa dreccendan D
60:1(3)	anxiaretur	nu me c̱aru beateð V:	bið genyrwyd C̄ and so BG, anguð wearð D, geangsummed wæs K
60:2(4)	a facie inimici	s̱tið wið feondum V:	of ansyne feondys C and so DGK, from etc. B

120

60:3(5)	tabernaculo	s̱elesgesceote V: getelde CB, eardunge DKG	
60:5(7)	adicies	a̱ndweard gangan V: togeicst C, geecest B, geic DKG	
60:5(8)	conspectu	a̱nsyne V: gesihðe CBDKG	
61:2(3)	movebor	f̱orhtige wiht V: onstyryd CB, astyred DKG	
61:3(4)	interficitis	to ḏeadan ḏædun V: ofsleað CBDK, ofsle(..) G	
61:3(4)	macherie	w̱ah of stofne V: wealle V, stanwealle BG, stangæderunga DK	
61:3(4)	inpulse (Ga. depulse)	aw̱urpon V: oncnyssyde C, gecnysedum BG and so D, gecyssed K	
61:4(5)	repellere	tow̱eorpan V: awegadrifan CB, anydan DKG	
61:6(7)	emigrabo	bef̱leon V: gefeore C, leore B, afeorrie D and so KG	
61:9(10)	mendaces	m̱anes unlyt V: lease CBDKG	
61:10(10)	sperare	gew̱enan V: hihten CBDKG	
62:2(2)	multipliciter	s̱wyðe V: mænigfealdlice C and so BDKG	
62:3(3)	in aquoso	w̱æterflodum V: on wætrige stowe C, wætregum B and so DKG	
62:7(7)	matutinis	æ̱rmergen V: morgynne C, on morgentid B, on dægredum D, in dæred K, ondægred/on uhttidum/on mergen G	
62:7(7)	stratum	ṟeste V: stræte C, strene B, bedd DKG	
62:8(8)	exultabo	hiht..ẖæbbe V: gystige C, gefeo B, blissige DKG	

121

62:9(10)	introibunt	e̲odon V: inngað CBDKG
62:9(10)	inferiora terræ	eorðscræfu V: nyðyrran eorðan C and so BDKG
62:10(12)	obstructum	synt ge̲myrde V: fortimbryde C and so B, fordytt DKG
63:1(2)	tribulor	me c̲otunge c̲nyssað V: geswencyd CBD, not in K or G
63:1(2)	eripe	ge̲scyld V: genere CB and so DG, alys K
63:2(3)	protexisti	aw̲erdest V: gescyldyst C and so B, bewruge DKG
63:2(3)	conventu malignantium	w̲yrigra gemotes V: gesomnunge awyrgendra CB, gemetinge wyrgendra DK, gemetinge of mænigeo G
63:3(4)	exacuerunt	teoð t̲eonan V: ascyrpton CB, hwetton DKG
63:3(5)	immaculatum	unsc̲yldige V: unwemman C and so BDKG
63:4(6)	dixerunt	s̲precað V: cwædon CBDKG
63:7(8)	sagittæ	s̲cytelum V: flana C, stræla BDKG
63:7(9)	nihilo	ne aw̲iht V: nowihte CA, fore noht B, is for naht D, not in K or G
63:9(11)	iusta	soðfæsta V: rihtwis CBDKG
64:2(3)	veniet	⨯s̲iðian V: cymyð C and so BDKG
64:3(4)	verba iniquorum	s̲ynfulra word V: word unrihtwisra CBDKG
64:3(4)	prevaluerunt	f̲oran V: strangydon CB, rihsodon DKG
64:3(4)	impietatibus	m̲isdædum V: arleasnyssum CBDKG
64:3(4)	propitaberis	ge̲fultuma V: gemyldsast C and so BDKG

122

64:4(5)	elegisti	g̲eceoseð V: gecure CBDKG	
64:7(7)	virtute	m̲ihte V: mægyne CBDKG	
64:7(8)	fundum maris	d̲eope wælas V: grund sæys C and so BDK, grunddeopon sæ G	
64:8(9)	signis	w̲undrum V: tacnum CBDG, ungl K	
64:8(9)	fines maris (Ga. terminos)	u̲tan landes V: endas eorðan CBD, gemæru G, ungl K	
64:9(9)	matutini	æ̲rmorgenes V: morgyntide/uhttide C, uhttide B, dægredes DG, ungl K	
64:10(10)	cibum	f̲eorhnere V: mete CBDKG	
64:11(11)	rivos	w̲æter yrnende V: rynylan CB, rynelas DKG	
65:2(3)	terribilia	w̲undorlice V: egesfulle CB, egeslicu DKG	
65:4(4)	filios hominum	y̲lda bearn V: bearn manna CB, suna manna DKG	
65:5(4)	convertit	mæg onw̲enden V: gecyrryð CB, gecyrde DKG	
65:5(6)	pertransibunt	g̲efeterian V: þurh leorað mid fet C, þurh leorað B, oferforan DKG	
65:5(6)	flumina	s̲treamas V: flodas CBDKG	
65:9(10)	probasti	c̲ostade V: acunnudyst C and so B, fandudest DK, fordydest G	
65:9(10)	examinasti	a̲seoðeð V: amearydest C and so BDKG	
65:10(11)	tribulationes	b̲ealuwa V: gedrefydnysse C, geswencednesse B, geswinc DKG	
65:11(12)	aquam	f̲loda þrym V: wætyr C and so BDKG	

65:12(13)	holocausta	tifer V: onsægdnysse C and so BDKG
65:13(15)	holocausta medulata	tifrum teala V: onsægdnysse mirilice C and so B, onsægdnissa geswetlæhta DKG
65:18(20)	amovit	dyde V: onwende C, aweg awende B, atyrde DK, lufode G
66:2(3)	cognoscamus	andgyt habbað V: oncnæpen C, oncnawan BDKG
66:4(5)	æquitate	on rihtum V: unrihwise K, efynnysse CBDG
66:6(8)	metuent	hæbbe..egesan V: ondrædon C and so BDKG
67:2(3)	peccatores	fyrenfullan V: synfulle CBDKG
67: 2(4)	iusti	soðfæste V: rihtwise C and so BDKG
67:3(4)	conspectu	ansyne V: K, gesihðe CBDK
67:3(4)	delectentur	habbað..blisse and sibbe V: syn gelustfullude CB, gegladien DG, gladiað K
67:7(7)	vinctos	gehæftan V: gebundyne CB and so DKG
67:7(7)	fortitudine	mihte V: strenge C, strengþu BK, strangnesse DG
67:7(7)	sepulchris	eorðscræfum V: byrgynnum C and so BDKG
67:8(8)	egredieris	gangeð V: utgæst CBDK, ungl G
67:11(11)	animalia	wihte V: nytenu CBDKG
67:11(11)	parasti	sealdest V: gearwodyst C and so BDKG
67:15(16)	montem	gebeorh V: munt CBDKG

67:18(19)	dedit dona	wæs lacgeofa V: sealde gife CB, sealde selena D, underfenge gyre K, onfenge sylena G	
67:21(22)	verticem capilli	feaxes scadan V: hnoll loccas CBDG, heafda K	
67:22(24)	intinguatur	weorðe fæste V: bedyppyd C and so BDKG	
67:26(31)	offerunt munera	gyfe lædeð V: offrydon gyfe C, bringað lac DKG, lac B	
68:1(2)	introierunt	floweð 7 gangeð V: ineodon CDKG, lac B	
68:6(6)	obscondita	bemiðene V: ahydde C, behydde DKG, lac B	
68:9(10)	zelus	heard ellenwod V: hatheortnys CBG, tyrging DK	
68:11(12)	posui	cyme cyrde V: sette CBDKG	
68:11(12)	vestimentum	gewæda V: hrægl CBD, scryd K, hrægl/reaf G	
68:11(12)	cilicium	witehrægl V: heran CBG, onhæran DK	
68:11(12)	parabolam	wæfersyn V: bispell CBDKG	
68:12(13)	exercebantur (Ga: loquebantur)	wiðerwearde wæron V: bieodon CB fliton D, spæcon K, spræcon G	
68:13(14)	veritate	hlutre V: soðfæstnesse CBDKG	
68:14(15)	libera	ado V: gefreo CB, alys DKG	
68:15(16)	urgeat	supe V: þregyþ C and so B, genyrwe DKG	
68:16(17)	respice	geseoh V: beseoh K, geloca CBD, geloca/beheald G	
68:17(18)	tribulor	feohtað V: beom geswencyd C and so BDKG	

68:19(20)	conspectu	ansyne V: K, gesihðe CBDG
68:19(21)	tribulantes	fæcne wurdon V: swencende CBDG, drefað K
68:20(21)	inveni	findan V: gemette CBD, onfunde K, oncom G
68:21(22)	dederunt	mengdan V: sealdun C and so BDKG
68:25(26)	habitatio	wic V: eardungstow C, eardung BDKG
68:26(27)	percussisti	earfoðu..geafe V: sloge CBDKG
68:27(28)	iustitiam	soðfæst weorc V: rihtwisnesse CBDKG
69:1(2)	festina	hraðe V: efst CBDK, efst/efesð G
69:3(4)	avertantur	hweorfað..cyrrað V: syn forcyrryde C and so B, syn gecerred DKG
69:3(4)	retrorsum	hinderlincg V: on bæc CB, underbecling DKG
70:1(2)	iustitia	swiþeran miht V: rihtwisnesse CBDK, unrihtwisnesse G
70:3(3)	refugium	fultumiend V: gebeorg CB, frofer /gener DG, frofer K
70:3(4)	manu	folum V: handa CBDKG
70:3(4)	peccatoris	firenwyrcendra V: synfullys C and so BDKG
70:5(6)	protector	þeccend V: gescyldynd C and so BDG, frofer K
70:8(9)	defecerunt	mylte V: aspringyð CB, aspr(..)gð G, ateorað DK
70:9(10)	custodiebant	sætendan V: heoldon CBDKG
70:9(10)	fecerunt	eodon V: dydon CBDKG
70:10(11)	eripiat	hæbbe helpend V: generge CBDG alyse K

70:11(12)	respice	be_seoh V: K, geloca CBD, beheald /loca G
70:12(13)	querunt	_syrwedan V: seceað C and so DKG, sohton B
70:12(13)	operiantur	byð _scand V: ofyrwrigyn C and so BDKG
70:14(15)	iustitiam	_mægenspede V: rihtwisnesse CBDKG
70:15(15)	cognovi	on_geat V: oncnew C and so BDK, oncreow G
70:18(16)	iustitiæ	_mære soð V: rihtwisnesse CBDKG
70:19(29)	tribulationes	_earfoðes V: geswencydnysse C, geswinc BDKG
70:20(21)	conversus	ge_hwyrfdest V: gecyrryd C and so BDKG
79:18(20)	faciem	_andwlitan V: ansyne C and so BDKG
84:4(5)	converte	ge_hweorf V: gecyrr C and so BDK, lac G
89:15(13)	convertere	ge_hweorf V: gecyr CBDKG
89:15(13)	deprecare (Ga. deprecabilis)	wes..wel eaðbene V: bide CB, halsa DK, bentiðe G
89:18(16)	respice	ge_seoh V: geloca CBDKG
94:4(4)	in manu	_healdeð V: on handa CDKG, on onwalde B
94:4(4)	montium	_heahbeorgas V: munta CBDKG
94:5(5)	fecit	_sette V: dyde CB, worhte DKG
94:6(6)	adoremus	_cneow bigeað V: weorðiyn C, gebidden B, uton gebiddan DKG
94:7(7)	pascue	_edisce V: læsive CB, fostornodes DG, heorde K

94:9(9)	exacerbationes	g̱rimnesse V: onscununge CB, (Ga. irritatione) gremminge DK, aheardian G	
94:10(10)	errant	ḫyge dysegedan V: dwoliað CBDKG	
94:11(11)	iuravi	aðe benemde V: swor CBDKG	
102:1(1)	nomen sanctum	ęcan naman V: naman haligne CBDKG	
102:2(2)	retributiones	ęalra goda V: edlean CBDKG	
102:3(3)	iniquitatibus	m̱andædum V: unrihtwisnesse CBDKG	
102:5(5)	coronat	gęsigefæste V: gebeagað CB, gewuldorbeagað DG, ungl K	
118:176	servum	ęsne ęlne V: þeow CB, þeowan DKG	
133:1(1)	servi	o̱nbyhtscealcas V: þeowas CBDKG	
133:4(3)	terram	ḫrusan V: eorðan CBDK, lac G	
148:2(2)	laudate	ḻofige V: hergeað C and so DKG, lac B passim 148-150	
148:2(2)	omnes angeli	ęngla ðreatas V: ealle englas CDKG	
148:4(4)	celos	w̱olcnum V: hefynas C and so DKG	
148:8(8)	ignis grando nix glacies	fy̱r fo̱rst hægel and gęfeallan snaw V: fyr hagol snaw is C, fyr storm snaw is DKG	
148:8(8)	faciunt	w̱yrcean V: doð CDKG	
148:14(14)	adpropianti (Ga. appropinquanti)	ṇeaweste V: genealæcendum CDKG	
149:7(7)	populis	ḫeowdum V: folce C and so DK (..)cum G	
149:8(8)	conpedibus	c̱ampum V: fotcopsum C, fotcopsum DKG	
150:1(1)	in firmamento	ƒhælu V: on trymnysse CDG, on embehwyrfte K	
150:3(2)	in sono	ḫleoðre V: on swege CDKG	

COMMENTARY ON COLLATION LIST 4X

24:3(4)   notas: K preserves a singular reading which
             may have been suggested by the Ga. text
             demonstra.

24:6(7)   iuventutis: V provides a phrase to round out the
             line, although the psalter-readings provide the
             appropriate alliteration.

34:2(2)   arma et scutum: V chooses gar for arma instead
             of wæpn for alliteration purposes. The partial
             lacuna in G is due to fire damage at fol. 41v.

34:3(3)   effunde: the lacuna in G is due to fire damage
             at fol. 41v.

34:3(3)   frameam: note the difference in readings between
             the A and D families.

51:7(10)   olivia: assuming that the line contains three
             alliterating words (ic, elebeam and up), V
             preserves a singular reading although the A and
             D traditions provide the necessary alliteration
             elements.

52:4(4)   declinaverunt: I am assuming that besegan is
             part of an "s" alliteration in an "A-Type" line
             with symle and soð in a "B-Type" line.

52:5(5)   iniquitatem: unless otherwise noted, V invaria-
             bly renders this as unriht.

52:5(5)   cognoscent: G follows the Ga. text sciant with
             hi ne witan, although placing it in the negative.

53:2(4)   verba oris mei: this is clearly poetic composi-
             tion in V to provide a vowel alliteration.

53:7(9)   eripuisti: V generally follows BDKG with genere
             for this lemma, but here substitutes alysdest
             for alliterative purposes.

54:12(15)   consensu: G preserves both the A and D readings.
             Note that the CB reading would have provided
             V with the appropriate alliteration.

54:23(24)   dimidiabunt: the D family differs considerably from CB.

55:6(7)   calcaneum: G preserves both the A and D readings. Any of the gloss readings would have provided V with the necessary alliteration.

55:8(10)   retrorsum: V and K accord together with a singular reading.

56:2(3)   deum altissimum: V uses elements from the psalter-glosses and inverts them for an "h"-alliterating line.

56:10(9)   psalterium: sealmleof in K is probably the result of erroneous copying of sealmleod in D.

57:3(4)   erraverunt: G preserves a singular reading.

57:4(6)   incantantur: K appears to follow the form of the Ga. text incantantis with ongalendra.

57:6(8)   intendit: notice that C, D and G accord, while B and K preserve unique readings.

58:2(3)   viris sanguinem: V uses elements from the psalter-glosses, but inverts word order and intensifies the modifier.

58:10(12)   obliviscantur: the gloss readings would have provided V with the necessary alliteration.

58:11(12)   protector: K preserves a singular gloss which is independent of both the A and D traditions.

58:12(13)   conpellantur: K and G follow the Ga. text.

58:13(14)   iacob: is this a hint of etymological interpretation in V?

58:16(17)   virtutem: V and K accord, possibly following the Ga. text fortitudinem. This does not, however, suggest that V was influenced by the Gallican Latin text but only, perhaps, by a gloss resulting from a direct (and therefore early) translation from the Ga. text.

59:4(5) significantionem: tacuga in K is probably a scribal error for the getacnunga gloss in the other psalters.

59:10(13) tribulatione, also tribulantes: D double-glosses this lemma with the common gloss rendering and with a singular reading.

61:3(4) interficitis: there seems to be a word play in V.

61:3(4) macherie: G follows CB, while DK provides a reading which is less translation than interpretation. The CBG gloss would have provided V with the appropriate alliteration.

61:6(7) emigrabo: leore in B may be from leordon which occurs elsewhere in B (cf. 65:11(12)).

62:3(3) in aquoso: the majority of the gloss readings provide the requisite alliteration, but probably too few syllables for V.

62:7(7) matutinis: G's triple gloss represents the A and D traditions, plus another reading, on uhttidum, which occurs elsewhere in B and C.

62:7(7) stratum: C and B differ, with the C reading being Latinate.

62:8(8) exultabo: C and B again differ from each other and both differ from DKG.

62:9(10) introibunt: the psalm-gloss readings would have provided V with the necessary alliteration.

63:1(2) tribulor: K and G follow the Ga. text.

63:1(2) eripe: gescyld in V may be the result of the A family's reading of gescyldyst for protexisti in the next verse.

63:2(3) conventu malignantium: Rosier attributes G's translation to a misreading by the glossator.

63:7(8) sagittæ: C preserves flana, which appears elsewhere in C and K, 56:5(5).

63:7(9)	<u>nihilo</u>: K and G follow the Ga. text.
64:2(3)	<u>veniet</u>: I have read this line as having a double alliteration, although the "f" sound takes precedence over the "s" sound.
64:4(5)	<u>elegisti</u>: I have accepted <u>geceosað</u> as providing a third alliterating word, although the "c" there is palatal, as opposed to the velar "c" of <u>cystum</u> and <u>clæne</u>.
64:7(8)	<u>fundum</u> <u>maris</u>: G preserves a singular reading.
64:8(9)	<u>fines</u> <u>maris</u>: G preserves a singular reading, perhaps following the Ga. text <u>terminos</u>.
64:9(9)	<u>matutini</u>: B renders the lemma as <u>uhttide</u> (cf. entry for <u>matutinis</u>, 62:7 above, for G's reading), while C shows a double gloss, whose first element is not unlike the reading in V, and whose second element is also <u>uhttide</u>.
65:4(4)	<u>filios</u> <u>hominum</u>: <u>ylda</u> <u>bearn</u> in V is an unusual reading, the common form being <u>manna</u> <u>bearn</u> after ABC.
65:10(11)	<u>tribulationes</u>: B accords in principle with DKG.
65:18(29)	<u>amovit</u>: <u>lufode</u> in G is an obvious error in direct translation.
66:4(5)	<u>æquitate</u>: although K appears to be close to V, its reading is in fact an error.
67:3(4)	<u>conspectu</u>: V and K accord with <u>ansyne</u>.
67:18(19)	<u>dedit</u> <u>dona</u>: K preserves a singular reading.
67:21(22)	<u>verticem</u> <u>capilli</u>: K preserves a singular reading.
68:11(12)	<u>vestimentum</u>: K preserves a singular reading, while G double-glosses the lemma with the CBD reading, and a unique gloss.
68:11(12)	<u>cilicium</u>: perhaps <u>witehrægl</u> in V was suggested by <u>hrægl</u>, in C, B or D for <u>vestimentum</u> in the same verse.

68:12(13)	exercebantur: K and G follow the Ga. text loquebantur.
68:19(21)	conspectu: V and K accord with ansyne.
68:19(21)	tribulantes: K preserves a singular reading which occurs elsewhere in C (cf. 65:10).
68:29(21)	inveni: oncom in G appears to be an effort at direct translation by a scribe with a poor knowledge of Latin.
70:1(2)	iustitia: unrihtwisnesse in G is a scribal error for rihtwisnesse.
70:3(4)	manu: V prefers the poetic word folmum (here and elsewhere, cf. 94:5) to the more common handa, which appears in 133:3(2) only to provide alliteration.
70:5(6)	protector: K preserves a singular reading.
70:8(9)	defecerunt: the partial lacuna in G's gloss which follows CB, is due to fire damage at fol. 70v.
70:10(11)	eripiat: K preserves a singular reading.
70:15(15)	cognovi: oncreow in G is a scribal error for oncneow.
84:4(5)	converte: the lacuna in G is due to fire damage at fol. 84r.
89:15(13)	deprecare: G preserves a singular reading. (Read eaðbede in Krapp, p.61).
89:18(16)	respice: read beseoh in Krapp, p.61.
94:4(4)	in manu: note B's unusual gloss here. The CDKG gloss would have provided V with the appropriate alliteration.
94:7(7)	pascue: K preserves a singular reading.
149:8(8)	conpedibus: note the metathesis on "sp"/"ps" between the A and D glosses.

150:1(1)   in firmamento: K preserves a singular reading. There appears to be a double alliteration here with "h" and "m", although the latter seems to be the primary one.

COLLATION LIST 4Y

5:1(2)	intellege	gehyr V: ongyt C and so BDKG
24:6(7)	delicta	fyrena V: scyld CB and so DKG
32:18(22)	fiat	wese V: sy C and so BDKG
43:27(26)	libera	ahrede V: gefreo CB, alys DKG
50:10(10)	averta	awend V: acyrr C and so BDKG
50:10(10)	dele	adwæsc V: adylga CB, dilga D and so KG
50:11(12)	crea	syle V: gecwica CB, scype DKG
50:12(13)	auferas	aber V: afyr C and so BDG, lac K
50:13(14)	redde	syle V: agyf C and so B, agyld DG. lac K
51:6(9)	speravit	getruwode V: gehihte C and so BDG, lac K
51:7(10)	fructifera	weaxende V: wæstmbære CBDG, lac K
52:3(3)	prospexit	beseah V: forðlocað C and so BG, gelocode D, lac K
52:6(6)	dissipat	tosceadeð V: tostenceað C and so BG, tosteneð D. lac K
52:7(7)	exultabit	byð on glædum sælum V: gefihþ CB, freaþaneað D, freoðað G, lac K

53:5(7)	disperde	toweorp	V: tostregd C, forspild B and so DK, generedest G
53:6(8)	sacrificabo	cweme	V: offrige CDKG, onsæge B
53:7(9)	respexit (Ga. despexit)	ofersawe	V: gelocode CB and so DK, forseah G
54:3(4)	declinaverunt	on sah	V: anhyldon C and so BDKG
54:8(10)	precipta	hat	V: forbred C and so B, afyl/ahyld DG, arful K
54:8(10)	vidi	locode	V: geseah CBDKG
54:8(10)	civitate	burgum	V: ceastre CBDKG
54:9(12)	iniustitiæ	unsoðfæstnys	V: unrihtwisnesse CBD, on rihtwisnesse KG
54:9(11)	circumdabit	þunie	V: ymbsylyð C and so BDKG
54:12(15)	capiebas	æton	V: name CBG, gripe DK
54:14(16)	nequitia	inwit	V: niþ CBDKG
54:20(22)	mollierunt (Ga. molliti sunt)	gesmyredon	V: gehnehsudon C and so BD, gehnexsud synd K and so G
54:21(23)	cogitatum	gehygd	V: hige K, geþoht CBD, not in G
54:23(24)	sperabo	getreowige	V: gehihte C and so BDKG
55:6(7)	confringes	geðreatast	V: gebrycyst CB, forbricst DKG
57:5(7)	conteret	gescæneð	V: forþræstyð CB forbryteð, DKG
58:4(5)	dirigebar (Ga. direxi)	geswac	V: wæs gereht CB, geriht wæs DKG
58:9(11)	preveniet	becom	V: forcymyð CB and so DKG

58:11(12)	disperge	todrif V: tostenc CDG, tostregd B, tostenge K
58:12(13)	conprehendantur	wærun..gescende V: beoð befongynne CB, syn gegripene DKG
58:15(16)	disperguntur	gewitað V: beoð tostencyde C, beoð tostrogdne B, tofarene beoð DKG
59:2(4)	commovisti	onhrerdest V: onstyrydyst C and so B, astyredes D and so KG
59:5(8)	convallem	Convallem V: gemære CBA, hole dene DK, deneland G
59:7(10)	subditi sunt	gewylde V: underðeodde synd CBDKG
60:4(6)	timentibus	se þe..fortað V: ondrædyndum CBDKG
61:3(4)	irruitis	mid mane..ongunnon V: onræsað C, hreosað BG, hreos geon D, yrsige K
61:8(9)	effundite	doð V: arotað C, ageotað BDKG
61:11(11)	apponere	staðelian V: tosettan CBDKG
62:7(7)	meditabor	gewene V: smeage CBKG, gemyndigge D
62:8(9)	adhesit	getreoweð V: ætfealh CB, togeþeodde DK, ongeþeodde G
63:5(7)	defecerunt	forweorðað V: asprungon CB, geteorodon DKG
63:8(10)	adnuntiaverunt	mærsian V: sædon C, cyððan B, bebodedon DG and so K
63:9(11)	sperabit	geweneð V: gehihtyð CBDKG
64:9(10)	inebrasti	gefyllest V: ofyrdrenctyst C and so BDKG
64:10(10)	flumen	streamas V: flod CBDK, lac G

64:12(12)	coronam	hring V: bieh C and so B, trendel DKG
64:12(12)	ubertate	wæstmum V: genihtsumnesse CBDKG
65:6(7)	respiciunt	wliteð V: gelociað CBDKG
65:6(7)	provocant (Ga. exasperans)	gebringað V: gegrymde CB, forðgecigað D, on yrre forðgæð K tyrwiað G
65:7(8)	obaudite (Ga.auditam)	asecgean V: hyrsumiað C and so B, hlystað DK, gehyrde G
65:8(9)	commovere (Ga. commotationem)	hreran V: onstyrgeanne C and so B, astyred D, styrunge K and so G
65:13(14)	tribulatione	þearfe V: geswencydnysse C, geswince BDK, ge(..) G
65:13(15)	offeram	forgulde V: onsecge C, ofrige BK, bringe DG
65:16(18)	conspexi (Ga. aspexi)	oncneow V: gelocode CB, geseah DKG
66:4(5)	dirigis	healdest V: gerecyst C and so BDG, ungl K
66:6(8)	fines	gemæru V: endas CBDKG
67:1(2)	dissipentur	toworpen V: tostencte C, tostroydne B, syn todræfed D and so KG
67:8(8)	mota est	onhrered V: onstyred CB, astyred is DKG
67:11(11)	inhabitabunt	lifiað V: oneardiað CBD, eardiað KG
67:13(14)	cleros	clero V: þreatas CB, gehlyttan DKG
67:14(15)	dealvabuntur	weorðað V: beoð gehwitte C, beoð ablicen BDKG
67:15(16)	pinguis	þicce V: fætt CBDKG

67:21(22)	perambulantium	eodon V: geongangyndra CB, gangendra D and so K, þurhgangendra G	
67:22(23)	convertam	onwende V: gecyrre CBDKG	
67:22(23)	profundum	deopre V: deopnesse K, grund CBDG	
67:27(31)	probati sunt	beoð..gecoste V: gecunnude C and so DKG, lac B	
67:28(31)	dissipa	toweorp V: tostenc CDK, tostengt G, lac B	
68:1(3)	infixus sum	oflegd V: gefæstnos C, afæstnod DK and so G, lac B	
68:2(2)	altitudinem	hricg V: heanysse C, deopnesse DKG, lac B	
68:3(4)	spero	gewene V: gehihte C and so DKG, lac B	
68:3(4)	defecerunt	wiðgangen V: asprungon C, geteorodon DKG, lac B	
68:4(5)	capillos	feaxes V: loccas CDG, heafdes K, lac B	
68:7(7)	revereantur (Ga. confundantur)	unare..findan V: onscuniyn C, forwandien D, forwyrþan K, secað G, lac B	
68:8(8)	operui (Ga. operuit)	aræfnade V: oferwrah CBDKG	
68:10(11)	operui	gesette V: ofyrwreah C and so BDKG	
68:12(13)	porta	on portum V: gatum CBDKG	
68:12(13)	psallebant	spræcon V: sungan CBDKG	
68:15(16)	profundum	deop V: d.opnes K, grund CBDG	
68:17(18)	faciem	gesyhð V: ansyne CBDKG	
68:23(24)	obscuretur	syn..adimmad V: syn aþustrude CBD, geþystrian K, sy onstyred G	

68:32(33)	lætentur	gefeoð V: blisiyn C and so BDKG
68:35(36)	civitates	byrig V: cestra C and so BDKG
69:3(4)	cogitant (Ga. volunt)	hogedon V: þenceað CBD, willað KG
70:1(1)	speravi	gewene V: hihte CBDKG
70:2(3)	protectorem	þeccend V: gescyldynd C and so BDKG
70:3(4)	eripe	alys V: genere CB, <u>ungl</u> D, nera KG
70:11(12)	elonges (Ga. elongeris)	ofgif V: afeorra CBD, feorsa K, afeorsa G
70:13(14)	sperabo	getreowige V: gehihte CBDKG
70:18(19)	fecisti	geworhtest V: dydest CBDKG
70:19(20)	reduxisti	alysdest V: gelæddyst CDKG, alæddes B
70:20(21)	multiplicasti	tobræddest V: gemonigfealodyst CB, mænigfyldest D and so K, gemænifyldyst/gemonigfealdodest G
70:22(24)	meditabitur	mærde V: smeagynde C, smeað BDKG
79:18(20)	converte	gehweorf V: gecyrr C and so BDK, ge(..) G
87:13(14)	preveniet	becume V: forcymð C and so BDKG
89:15(13)	servos	scealcum V: þeowas CB þeowan DKG
94:1(1)	exultemus	herigean V: gefeon CB, blissian DKG
94:2(2)	preoccupemus	secean V: abisgiyn C and so B, ofðriccen DKG
94:5(5)	fundaverunt	worhte V: gestaþelodon CBD, gelogude K, gescopan G

118:176	non sum oblitus	forgeat V: forgiten K, ofyrgettu C, ofergitoliende B, ofergyten DG
148:5(4)	mandavit	het V: bebead CDKG, lac B pass. 148-150.
148:6(6)	statuit	staðelade V: gesette CDKG
148:6(6)	preteribit	heoldon V: beleorde forðeode C, leoreð D, forþgewit K, forhogude G
148:9(9)	colles	geswyru V: hyllas C, beorgas D, ungl K, h(...) G
148:9(9)	ligna	beamas V: treow C and so DKG
148:12(12)	iuvenes	hægestealdas V: iunge CDKG
149:2(2)	filie	bearn V: dohtra CDKG
149:2(2)	exultent	hihtan V: gefeon CA, fægnian DKG
149:5(5)	cubilibus	husum V: bedcleofum C, incleofum DKG
149:7(7)	nationibus	cynnum V: cneorissum C, mægþum DKG
150:2(2)	magnitudinis	mægenþrymmes V: micylnysse C and so DKG

COMMENTARY ON COLLATION LIST 4Y

53:5(7)   disperde: G's reading is probably the result of miscopying.

53:6(8)   sacrificabo: note the singular reading in B.

54:9(12) iniustitiæ: on rihtwisnesse in KG is the result of miscopying, but is not present in D.

59:5(8)   convallem: V renders this lemma incorrectly as a proper name, while G may be using etymological interpretation.

61:3(4)	irruitis: K preserves a singular reading.
61:8(9)	effundite: the C reading appears to be erroneous, and may be the result of miscopying.
64:10(10)	flumen: the lacuna in G is due to damage at fol. 64v.
65:6(7)	provocant: the reading in G also appears at 67:7(7), again glossing provocant.
67:13(14)	cleros: note the Latinate reading in V.
67:21(22)	perambulantium: the CB gloss appears here as a good example of a compound OE. invention to gloss a Latin lemma literally.
67:22(23)	profundum: V accords with K.
68:12(13)	porta: note the Latinate reading in V.
68:15(16)	profundum: K agrees with V although its gloss is incomplete.
79:18(20)	converte: the lacuna in G is due to fire damage at fol. 81v.
89:15(13)	servos: read scealcas in Krapp, p.61.
118:176	non sum oblitus: V and K show singular accordance.

Chapter IV: Conclusions and Postulations

Conclusions

From the foregoing tabulation lists, it becomes readily apparent that between two-thirds and three-quarters of the readings from V listed here, accord in some form with the psalter-glosses. In addition to this, the commentaries indicate instances in which not just a gloss, but an independent gloss is duplicated or echoed in V. From this evidence, it would seem fair to suggest a definite interlinear glossed psalter influence at work on the composition of the Old English metrical psalter. The following pages will examine this suggestion, clarifying and amplifying some of the points outlined in the commentaries.

The actual gloss traditions are less easy to establish than the fact of the influence itself. The greatest number of accordances between V and the psalter-glosses appears in Lists 3XY, which tabulate V's agreement with both the Vespasian and Regius families. If there is any Vespasian influence at all in the Regius Psalter, this result would seem inevitable. Thereafter, V's accordance with the Vespasian psalters C and B covers a greater number of readings than V's accordance with the Regius psalters D and G. Again, given the suggested purpose of D as an educational text, with its many unglossed words, as opposed to the more complete interlinear glosses found in the Cambridge or Junius book, this result is not surprising.

For the Vespasian family, we should first look at some of the readings in V which appear on List 1X but are not under alliterative restriction, that is, those readings whose choice by the V-poet was not determined by a required alliteration in the line. As the commentary notes, miserationum 24:5(6), adiuva 43:27(26), adiutorem 51:6(9), fortitudinem 58:9(10), superbia 58:12(13), finium terræ 58:13(14), adiutor 58:17(18), adiuva 69:6(6) and prodigium 70:6(7) fall into this category. Adiuva, adiutor, fortitudinem and miserationum are all rendered in the A and D families by glosses which provide the same initial alliteration sounds: for example, adiuva is glossed gefultuma by the Vespasian family, gefylst by the Regius group, both of which would contribute an "f"-alliteration to V. The adiuva-adiutor selection can be grouped together as a predictable vocabulary rendering in V which consistently accords with the A-family. Similarly, miserationum and fortitudinem are consistently translated by myldsa and strengðe in V, in accordance with the Vespasian family, rather than by miltsunga and strangnesse, as we find in the Regius glosses.

Finium terræ, *superbia* and *prodigium* all include compound elements such that the "choice" by the V-poet of the A-reading, lies in a part of each compound which is not affected by alliteration. Hence, *prodigium* is rendered *forebeacen* by V and the *Vespasian* family, and *foretacen* by the *Regius* group: yet the alliteration for that line in psalm 70:6 centers on an "f" sound, and therefore it is the prefix "*fore*" and not the substantive word-core "*beacen*" which carries the stress. From this we can see that either the A- or D-reading would supply the V line with the necessary alliteration, and so we must regard V's choice of the *Vespasian* over the *Regius* gloss as significant.

Filios hominum, first encountered in our study at 52:6(9), is rendered *bearn manna* by the *Vespasian* family, as opposed to *suna manna* by the *Regius* group. V takes the A-gloss, inverts word order, generally for metrical purposes, and maintains that reading throughout the remaining fragments, except for specific cases which the commentary has noted. Similarly, V invariably renders *improperium* or *obprobrium* as *edwit*, following the *Vespasian*, rather than the *Regius* gloss.

The other similarities are readily apparent from reading the tabulation lists and commentaries on them. It is, however, important to note here that certain of these similarities are for the most part consistent throughout the Old English metrical Psalter. *Cecidit* 54:4(5) is generally *feallað* in V, according with the A-gloss, while the D-family generally renders it as *hreas*. *Oderat* 54:11(13) is commonly glossed *feodon* by the V and the A-family, while the D-group reads *hatude* throughout. *Puteum* 54:22(24) is always *seað* in V and the A-family, while the *Regius* glosses render it *pytt*. *Dixit* or *narravit*, as in 54:16(18), are often *secge* in V and the A-group, but *cyðe* in the D-family, and *potestas* 61:12(12) is generally *miht* or *mægen* in V, *miht* in the *Vespasian* family, but *anweald* in the D-group. There are many other examples in both lists of these vocabulary "ranges" in V and the A- and D-glosses which underline the partial dependence of the Old English metrical Psalter on the *Vespasian* tradition.

List 1Y provides those readings in V which accord with the A-family and do not alliterate at all. As we have already seen, it also contains lemmata which are rendered in V, throughout the Psalter, to accord with the *Vespasian* tradition. In List 1Y too, we find repeated, some of the lemmata which in List 1X were not under alliterative restriction for reasons mentioned above: *adiuvat* 53:4(6), *auxilii* 61:8(8), and the like.

The presence of these readings in the 1Y list re-emphasizes the fact that the V-poet did not choose them in List 1X just for alliterative purposes. The entries in List 1Y are therefore significant, since alliteration plays no part in the preference in V for the Vespasian rather than the Regius tradition, and we must hence assume direct influence of one sort or another.

Yet we must not lose sight of the fact that the Vespasian gloss was a far older and more established one than that of the Regius Psalter at the time of the writing of V. Whether there is or is not Vespasian influence on D is a matter for either conjecture or a more detailed study than this, but it is safe to expect a greater percentage of V/A correspondences than of V/D correspondences, if only because of D's incomplete glosses. Yet, before turning to Lists 2X and 2Y, we must look at the sub-lists 1X-C, 1X-B, 1Y-C and 1Y-B, since in certain instances the Vespasian Psalter does not accord with the V readings. Generally, when V and C accord and B differs from them, the Vespasian Psalter agrees with B and not C. Similarly, when V and B accord, and C differs from them, the Vespasian Psalter agrees with V and B. This would seem to bear out Sherman Kuhn's assertion that B was copied directly from A in Winchester in the early tenth century. Yet this relationship should not be considered an indication of C's independence from A, since in certain cases (listed in 3X1 and 3Y1), A and C accord in a singular reading, but should be treated as a reinforcement of Brenner's original claim of B's dependence on A. The exact relationship of A and C is less easily definable than that of B and A, perhaps because the C-gloss was written a century later than the B-gloss.

As we have already noted in the introductions to Lists 2X and 2Y, the entries found therein are less immediately identifiable as accordances between V and D than were those entries of Lists 1X and 1Y, showing agreement between V and the A-family. Yet they are interesting to this study for their very peculiarity.

In some cases, there is simple agreement, as in nocentes mei 34:1(1): in others, we find a variation in the psalter-gloss readings, so for dic we read sæge as usual in V, but sege in DKG and cweð in the A-family. Most of the similarities, however, are either obscure errors in interpretation, common to both V and the Regius glosses, or readings which are more, rather than less, related. As example of this latter case, we find spolia 67:12(13) rendered as weorðlic reaf in V.

147

The Regius reaflac approaches the metrical Psalter reading more readily than does heryreaf from CB. Similarly, absconderem is rendered hyde in V and hydde in DK: G and the two Vespasian psalters add a prepositional prefix which lessens the likelihood of a traceable influence.

We should here again note that K and G, like virtually all of the psalter-glosses other than A, B, D, L or M, are too late to have influenced the actual composition of V directly. They have however been included in this study as having perhaps prototypes which may have played a significant role in influencing the writing of V. G, too is unreliable as a typical Regius gloss because of its inordinate number of double or triple-glossed lemmata. We see one important entry, where V and D accord alone: aliquantulum 89:15(13), where G and K follow their Gallican text, and C and B preserve a different reading. Therefore it should always be to the reading in D itself, rather than K or G, that we look first in considering the Regius-influenced entries of Lists 2XY.

There are other examples of the "nearer-rather-than-farther" accordances between V and the D-family, some of these being tabernaculis 64:4(5), letabor 59:5(8), terribilis 65:4(5), cedri 148:8(9), convertantur 58:6(7), and pusillo animo 54:7(9). Of this last we should say something. Modes mindom in V is closer to medmiclum mode in D than to lytyllmodum in the Vespasian glosses or medmiclum gast in K and G, although it certainly is not an exact accordance.

However, the most significant evidence of the influence of D upon V comes in the independent readings common to both. Timor et tremor is rendered egsa me and fyrhtu in V which copies the "error" in D (the first element of a double gloss for tremor, reading fyrhto) and the subsequent "error" in K. We must note also that, while this entry is included on List 2X, the alliterating word in the line is egsa and not the individual fyrhtu: hence alliteration was not the reason for V's choice of the D-reading. Similarly, tempestate is rendered mægenes hreoh in V, but mægenes takes the alliterator stress rather than hreoh, which follows hreohnisse of DK rather than storm in CB: this similarity, while not an "error" like the fyrhtu/tremor correspondence in V and D, shows a phrase, like the egsa me and fyrhtu rendering, which is under only partial alliterative restriction. We find it repeated at 68:2(2), where hreoh does take the alliterator stress in V.

Venefici 57:4(6) from List 2Y, shows C and B erroneously glossing the lemma as *gealdorcræftas*, while V follows the correct *Regius* reading as closely as metrical requirements permit. However, with the lemma phrase *cucurri in sitim, ore suo benedicebant* 61:4(5), V follows the misinterpretation of the D-glosses which assume that *sitim* goes with *ore*. The *Vespasian* glosses "punctuate" the line correctly as the entry shows.

Perhaps the most interesting reading in these lists comes at 59:5(8), when V renders the verb *metibor* as a proper name, *Metiboris*. This is not extraordinary in the Old English metrical Psalter, for the poet's Latin is weak and he makes other similar errors, especially in this particular psalm with its many foreign names. However, the *Regius Psalter*, together the *Junius Psalter* and imitated by the *Salisbury Psalter*, leaves this verb unglossed as it does for other proper names. G, C and A translate it properly as a verb: *metui* or *amete*. Two points emerge from this study: the first stems from the familiarity of the D-glossator with etymological interpretation for homiletic, or didactic glossing. If he thought that *metibor* was a proper name, why did he not try to interpret it? The only answer that I can find is that he does leave other, unfamiliar names unglossed (*Galaad*, *Idumea* and *Manasses* of the same psalm) and that, relying on Sisam's suggestion of D as a learning book, if he had known that *metibor* was a translateable part of speech, he would probably have tried to translate it.

The second point deals with the relationship here of B and D. They rarely accord without a general accordance of glosses (*alies* for *eripe* in both is an exception, and mention has been made of this in the commentary), but it is possible that the glossators made the same error independently of one another in supposing *metibor* to be yet another foreign name. Although B and D have both been assigned to Winchester, I think it unlikely that a similar provenance is explanation enough for a single accordance in an unusual case like this, esepcially considering that at least twenty-five years had elapsed between the writing of the B-gloss, and that of the D-gloss.

It is of course possible that the V-poet also came to his decision on *metibor* independently of the B- or D-glossator, but this would suggest that he was working with the Latin text alone, rather than with at least two, and probably more, glossed psalters. This error, then, coupled with the various other erroneous accordances, provides what would appear to be concrete evidence in favor of some influence, by a Regius-type gloss, on the composition of the Old English metrical Psalter.

The great number of entries in Lists 3X and 3Y provides overwhelming evidence of general psalter-gloss influence on V. Some of the accordances are tempered in V by metrical restrictions or compositional tendencies, such as the rendering of in vanitate 51:6(9) by on idel gylp in V, rather than on idylnesse of the psalter-glosses. Some of the readings, too, approach the "nearer-rather-than-farther" accordances of Lists 2XY, but in these cases the V reading differs equally from the Vespasian and Regius traditions, which may be said to accord with it to a similar degree. Examples of this are deargentate 67:13(14), where V reads fægeres seolfres (with the stress on fægeres), while the Vespasian-type glosses read besylfryde and the Regius tradition reads ofersylfrede; and contradictionem 54:8(10), where a similar relationship among the psalter-glosses and V occurs. I have noted these instances in the commentaries, and would draw the reader's attention to them for further study.

Naturally, with so many readings common to the Vespasian and Regius glosses, it would seem impossible to rule out Vespasian influence on the Regius family. I have extended the bounds of this putative influence by taking the liberty of assigning gloss traditions to V, designated "TRAD:A", "TRAD:D" and "TRAD:A/D" when considering the readings in Lists 3X1 and 3Y1. This is not to attempt to prove such an influence, or even to assume it, but merely to identify what appears to lie behind the readings of V in entries where they accord with most, but not all of the psalter-glosses.

Metrical requirements, mentioned above, are the main force behind the variance between V and the psalter-glosses and, coupled with compositional tendencies, are the cause of the singular readings in V, tabulated in Lists 4X and 4Y. We see inversion for metrical reasons (spiritum rectum 50:11(12) or patris orfanorum 67:5(6)), additional words or expansion to a phrase for metrical and alliterative purposes (molesti erant 54:3(4) or multiplica generationes 64:11(11)), word contraction for metrical reasons (veritatem 56:4(4)), or word form alteration for line stress (mendacio 58:12(13)). The examples of these metrically-based changes are recorded in detail in the commentaries of both the 3XY and 4XY list sets, but in the former, the readings in V are morphologically the same as those in the psalter-glosses, while in the latter they are different.

The readings in Lists 4XY account for little more than one quarter of the total readings tabulated. Therefore the probability of an influence existing between the psalter-glosses and the Old English metrical Psalter is three to one. In many cases, we find readings which are composition rather than translation, and in other instances it may be possible to posit a lost tradition, which might also account for some of the double-glosses which occur in the psalter-glosses as well.

Considering the stemma proposal of Frank Berghaus, we see that he postulated both the unidentified "Z" additions of Sisam, and a now-lost "Y" tradition of his own. But this "Y" source connects only with the Vespasian element in Eadwine"s Canterbury Psalter, and has no extended influence on the Cambridge, Regius, Salisbury or Vitellius glosses. For example, Berghaus includes G in only his A and D stemmata which he fuses at the center of his chart to illuminate the genealogy of E, but it is quite possible that a now-lost, but more generally-influential tradition existed, and that it may have accounted for the unusual readings in G or C, or for some of the V readings included in Lists 4XY. This is no more than mere conjecture for the Old English metrical Psalter, since we find no remarkable accordances between the unusual gloss elements of G or C, and V which might stem from a common ancestor. Nevertheless, such a possible consideration should be made in light of the number of glossed books which must have existed in England.[1] On those entries in which the psalter-gloss readings would have provided V with the necessary alliteration, we can only speculate as to the motives of the poet at work: however, from the foregoing pages, we can say with a fair degree of certainty that psalter-gloss influence is clearly present in the Old English metrical Psalter.

There is also the matter of the occasional accordance between V and K in Lists 4XY, as well as the prevalence in K of singular readings, or the sporadic adherence of K to the Vespasian tradition when agreeing with V in the earlier lists. While technically a Regius psalter-gloss, the translation of K preserves many singular and unusual readings which have been duly noted in the commentaries to the different lists. They include slight modifications (specende is for locutus est 59:5(8) instead of sprecende is), readings which slightly resemble those of the other psalter-glosses (lædere for dux, 54:12(14), instead of ladþeow), or readings which differ totally from the others (on behæsc for in promisione, 55:7(9) instead of on gehate, or wæxt for lavabit, 57:9(11) instead of ðwyhð). Some of K's readings are unique, such as the rendering of Juda as christus, 59:7(9), clearly the result of etymological interpretation, or the odd term glimædina which it shares with E alone, 67:24(26). In places K preserves a reading which occurs as part of a double gloss in D or G, perhaps the result of a copying tradition suggesting a number of "interim" books among these three psalters. In other places K accords with unexpected psalter-gloss readings, such as its accordance with the A-family for sagittent 63:3(5), or its agreement here with C for arma et sagittæ, 56:5(5).

Nevertheless it is important to notice that K will often accord with V where no other psalter shows the slightest agreement. Retrorsum 55:8(10), virtutem 58:16(17), æquitate 66:4(5), conspectu 67:3(4), and 68:18(29), respice 70:11(12), cogitatum 54:21(23), profundum 67:22(23) and 68:15(16), and non sum oblitus 118:176, are all readings from Lists 4X and 4Y in which V and K accord alone. It is perhaps significant to note that, unlike other "sets" of accordances (V with the A- or D-family), no groups such as the adiuva-adiutor combination can be formed from the list above. We find only two lemmata, conspectu and profundum, which appear twice.

When we consider, too, that despite being technically a Regius psalter-gloss, K will often follow the Vespasian pattern when according with V, we should begin to formulate the first attempts at identifying the specific psalter-gloss tradition behind the Old English metrical Psalter. The V-poet appears to have depended upon both glossing traditions for his material: he probably relied upon the Vespasian-type gloss more readily than upon the Regius-type, for the reasons already outlined. I suggest that he used no less than three interlinear glossed psalters as source books, shifting among them and perhaps depending on one gloss until it failed to supply him with an adequate alliteration. There is of course no possible way of identifying specific psalters as sources, since so many have been lost, but I would suggest that the V-poet used what Sisam calls a "D^k-type" psalter, that is, a Regius-type psalter which is a predecessor of K.[2] I propose this, since V shows virtually no identification with the Winchester Gallicanum group, outside of their relationship to the Regius Psalter, and since K preserves the independent accordances with V outlined above, as well as accordances with both V and D. It is difficult to conjecture about the other psalters used in this exercise, other than to suggest that they were Vespasian types. There is not a distinct enough accordance over a wide enough range of psalms to point to either the Cambridge or Junius Psalter with any evidence at all, but, as C and B each represent a different branch of the A-family,[3] and as there is a certain, although limited amount of singular accordance between V and each book, I propose that C- or B-prototype glosses were available to the poet for his work. This would seem to suggest the existence of the two gloss traditions, Vespasian and Regius, as well as that of the two Latin texts, Romanum and Gallicanum, in the same location at the same time. We must therefore assume that a center with a sizeable library is the provenance of the Old English metrical Psalter, and move from conclusion to postulation to provide a date, place of origin, and intention with which to round off our study of V.

Postulations

     Having proposed a definite psalter-gloss influence on V, I feel it necessary to follow such a conclusion with suggestions as to the date and place of origin for our Old English metrical Psalter. Provenance is more likely to suggest dating than would be the case vice versa, and so I postulate a place of composition for V on the strength of the following argument, hoping that it may, in turn, provide a clue for the date of V's composition.

     In a tentative proposal for word geography study, Helmut Gneuss has suggested that a certain group of Winchester manuscripts which may be identified with the Tenth Century Reform, displays what he terms "Winchester words". He examines specific manuscripts, including the Old English Benedictine Rule and the Regius Psalter, and draws conclusions about the place of D in this Winchester group, as follows:

> The Old English Benedictine Rule thus clearly represents an intermediate, but rather advanced stage between an older, partly unsettled usage and that of the Winchester group. There is another ms. which seems to hold a similar position in the development of vocabulary usage: this is BM Royal 2 B v, a Latin psalter with an Old English interlinear gloss, written about the middle of the tenth century, perhaps at the New Minster, Winchester, or at the Nunnaminster.[5]

Gneuss establishes a word-list, of which certain entries are pertinent to our study. As he shows, D displays a significant number of "Winchester words" which, according to the tabulation lists, are not reproduced in V: sunu in D is always bearn in V; gelaðung in D is cyrice in V; gylt in D, which also occurs in C, is translated scyld in V; þæð does not occur in V, but we find siðfæt instead; cnapa in D is cniht in V, ælþeodig or ælfremed in D is fremde in V; and the loan-words chor and cantic in D are rendered þreat and lofsang in V. Two Winchester words and their variations are used interchangeably in V: we find both the Winchester word miht, and mægen to translate "strength", and the verbs (ge)blissian, termed a Winchester word, and (ge)fægnian to translate "rejoice". Hence we are left with a selection of readings from D which would have facilitated both our study of psalter dependence and our quest for a provenance for V, were they to have appeared in the Old English metrical Psalter as well. The presence of only two Winchester words, and that in company with their non-Winchester counterparts, provides us with no evidence at all.

Yet we must not lose sight of the all-important fact that V is, after all, a poem rather than a prose piece. This brings us back to the original criterion behind the collations of this dissertation: alliterative restriction. A before we rule out a provenance on the grounds provided by Gneuss's suggestions, we should bear in mind the following consideration:

> It is important to distinguish words and forms that could arise in the course of transmission from century to century, or from dialect to dialect, from those that are structural in the verse, i.e., necessary to the metre.[6]

In his "Dialect Origins in the Earlier Old English Verse", Kenneth Sisam establishes this criterion which can be applied to our study of the Old English metrical Psalter and its provenance. His comments on the actual restriction of the alliterative line apply directly to the language of V, especially since Sievers[7] has noted that it contains certain Anglian forms. Yet Sisam provides a satisfactory explanation for this evidence:

> The chief difficulty lies in the
> artificial, often archaic vocabulary
> of Anglo-Saxon alliterative poems,
> whatever may be the period or dia-
> lect which produced them. The
> technique and style of the verse
> kept the poet hunting for synonyms
> or variant expressions, and encourages
> the persistence of set phrases. Hence
> many poetic words are not found in
> prose at all, and many compounds are
> hardly conceivable except in poetic
> diction. If then some words of an
> early poem occur in the prose of one
> dialect only, it cannot safely be
> argued that the poem was composed
> in that dialect.[8]

Sisam takes as example of this statement, the debate between Menner and himself over the Anglian words in Solomon and Saturn[9], to show that the presence (or absence) of specific vocabulary is not evidence enough on which to base a suggestion of original dialect in "early" poems. Although V is not early by Sisam's standards, the same indication would apply, and we may see that, although the Regius Psalter contains specific Winchester words, there is no reason why they will necessarily re-appear in a poetic paraphrase which used D as a source of some sort. Alliterative restriction remains the criterion by which poetic choice is generally made, a statement which reaffirms the importance of those entries in the non-alliterating, or "Y" lists of tabulation.

Similarly, should we in fact postulate Winchester as the place of origin for V, there is still no reason why the Winchester words of prose should appear in the language of poetry:

> A poet might prefer to take his
> models from the common stock rather
> than from the less-known work of
> his own district. In this way poems
> could be produced that do not belong
> to any local dialect, but to a general
> Old English poetic dialect, artificial,
> archaic, and perhaps mixed in its
> vocabulary, conservative in inflexions
> that affect the verse structure, and
> indifferent to non-structural

>   irregularities, which were perhaps
>   tolerated as part of the coloring
>   of the language of verse.[10]

And while the dependence of the Old English metrical Psalter upon the interlinear glossed psalters has been clearly esttablished by the evidence of Chapter III, we must nevertheless bear in mind that V is still a poem, and that therefore it will probably fall heir to something of this general Old English poetic dialect which Sisam outlines. Thus, while V is neither early nor strictly adherent to the alliterative pattern, we should not assume that a poetic paraphrase will necessarily display a vocabulary similar to that of prose, although it may be the product of the same scriptorium. This again underlines the significance of the accordances which we do find between V and the collated psalter-glosses. Equally, since V relies not only on D and its family, but also on the Vespasian tradition, as well as on some degree of original composition, we should not expect to find prevalence of "Winchester words" in its psalms.

Yet, with all of this in mind, Winchester still appears to be the most plausible provenance to suggest for the Old English metrical Psalter. The Junius and Regius Psalters have both been assigned to Winchester, and we have seen that each has some form of influence, direct or indirect, on V. Winchester, too, was the home of Æthelwold's school which would have possessed a library large enough to preserve more than one psalter of more than one textual or gloss tradition. Winchester was the court seat of Edgar, the royal patron of the Benedictine Reform, and was the site of the Regularis Concordia Synod of ca 972, at which Edgar and Æthelwold were present.

Winchester was also probably a major "distributing" center for the dissemination of manuscripts and learning. We have seen that Bodleian MS Junius 121 was written at Worcester ca 1075[11]: yet the other manuscript which preserves Benedictine Office fragments, Corpus Christi College, Cambridge 201, has also been assigned to Worcester, but from ca 1050[12]. This would mean that the original vernacular Office was complete by the mid-eleventh century, and indeed, if we accept Wulfstan as the compiler[13], the Office must have been composed within the first quarter of the eleventh century. We have also seen that the Paris Psalter was written in the southwest of England ca 1025[14]. Therefore, copies of the complete Old English metrical Psalter must have found their way to the southwest and to Worcester within sixty years of the writing of D which influenced it, probably within fifty years of the composition of V itself.[15] It is therefore likely that these copies were made in, and disseminated from the original place of writing. It is Winchester which lends itself admirably in terms of location, cultural and social importance, and scholarly resources, as the provenance of the Old English metrical Psalter.

Since the dating of V by the Menologium is very uncertain,[16] I would suggest a series of termini by which we may gradually bring into focus a plausible date for the writing of our metrical Psalter.

If the original[17] of D is the product of Dunstan's regime at Glastonbury and D is written shortly after 964[18], V would have to have been composed between 964 and 1025. If it is written in Winchester, it must have been earlier rather than later in that period, since learning improved vastly with the scholarship of such as Ælfric (at Winchester ca 980), and we have already seen that the Latin of the V-poet is inadequate and faulty. Since the Benedictine Reform saw its "upswing" during the reign of Edgar to 975, after which time the problems of succession and other matters disrupted the general impetus, I would propose the assignment of V to the age of what might be termed "Benedictine Celebration", the reign of Edgar himself. This then sharpens our termini to 964 and 975.

We must next examine the question of the motivation behind the writing of the Old English metrical Psalter. Such an undertaking was not likely to be a private project, but more probably a commissioned work. Therefore we may tentatively propose that an endeavor of this kind was commissioned either for, or by a figure of social importance, possibly the king himself. If such a project were commissioned for presentation to the king, we must needs look for a commissioner. The Church suggests itself as the most likely place of origin for such an undertaking: yet surely an ecclesiastical official such as Æthelwold of Winchester would have chosen a poet whose Latin did credit to his school as well as to his monastic order. As we have seen, the Latin of the V-poet is uneven, and might not have recommended him, as creator of a poetic paraphrase of the Latin Psalter, to a teacher as stern and scholarly as Æthelwold.[19] Similarly, the Church officials at Winchester would never have countenanced the obvious reliance upon the outdated Romanum text rather than the newly-standardized Gallicanum version which was in turn a result of the poet's need to rely upon gloss translations. Therefore, if we can rule out the Church as instigator of the writing of V, we should perhaps suggest that it was a lay person of importance, possibly Edgar, himself, who commissioned the work.

If V was the result of a commissioned work, it may have been intended for private devotions. Morrell[20] has suggested that the Paris Psalter was a devotional manuscript designed for some nobleman or noblewoman of the time, on account of its grand format. Yet the fact remains that the Old English metrical Psalter is in alliterative meter, a form which certainly lent itself to being read aloud at one stage of preConquest literary history. And while V's alliteration renders it a difficult piece to recite, we must bear in mind in this age of Benedictine Reform that the function of the Psalter was to be read aloud in the Benedictine Opus Dei. I would therefore suggest that the Old English metrical Psalter was probably intended for oral recitation, perhaps in imitation of earlier courts where alliterative verse may have been read aloud.

To recapitulate the points pertinent to a conclusion for our examination of V, we can safely assume a considerable degree of influence of the interlinear glossed psalters on the composition of the Old English metrical Psalter. This influence came from both the Vespasian and Regius families, with the latter most probably represented by a D^K-type psalter-gloss: and the Latin text which the V-poet indirectly used was the Roman, and not the Gallican version.

The most suitable provenance for V would appear to be Winchester, because of its location, and its social, educational and ecclesiastical predominance in Wessex. Since copies of V were available in Worcester and in the southwest of England within sixty years of the establishment of Æthelwold's Winchester school, we may also suggest Winchester both as a likely library for the V-sources, and as a plausible center for the distribution of these copies, reaffirming it as the most probable place of origin for V.

We have used conjecture in dating V and in establishing intention behind it, but the termini of 964 and 975 seem, in all likelihood, to be the most accurate for our purposes. V as a project appears to be a commissioned work, but it is not an educational endeavor because of the need for an intermediate source in translating the Latin of the Psalter. With this, and the foregoing in mind, we may suggest that it was perhaps the king himself, as patron of the Reform, who proposed the poetic paraphrase of the Psalter.

Therefore we may see the effect of the Benedictine Reform at work in the field of Old English poetry. Just as vernacular versions were made of the official documents of Benedictinism, the <u>Regula Sancti Benedicti</u> and later the <u>Regularis Concordia</u>, so the official liturgical basis of Benedictinism, the Psalter of the <u>Opus Dei</u>, was turned to vernacular verse in the early years of Benedictine revival. Yet the direct influence of the liturgy is present in this poetic paraphrase not just through intention, but in actual transmission, by virtue of its dependence on the interlinear glosses of the psalters which remain to us from the period. And this fact, when connected with the evidence of an increase in psalter-glossing during the period 964-1050, underlines the importance of the Old English metrical Psalter as a result of the Tenth Century Reform, as well as that of the relationship between liturgy and poetry of that era.

It is surely significant that a vernacular metrical psalter, was composed, perhaps in Winchester, with the use of interlinear glossed psalters, at a time when the Benedictine Rule was translated to vernacular prose, and Benedictinism was reviving throughout southern England. I have therefore tried to show to what extent these liturgical and educational glossed psalters, products of that revival, played a part in the unprecedented composition of a vernacular metrical psalter, so that we may begin to understand the relationship between liturgy and poetry in preConquest England.

NOTES

1. K. and C. Sisam, eds. The Salisbury Psalter, p.75.

2. Ibid., p.17.

3. cf. the stemmata developed by Frank Berghaus, Figure 1 in Chapter II of this dissertation.

4. Helmut Gneuss, "The Origin of Standard Old English and Æthelwold's School at Winchester", Anglo-Saxon England 1 (1972), pp.63-83.

5. Ibid., p.79.

6. cf. E. Sievers, "Zur Rhythmik des germanischen Alliterationverses", Beiträge 10 (1885), pp.474 and 483. Minnie C. Morrell, in her Manual of Old English Biblical Materials (Knoxville: 1965), deals with this question peripherally on page 141. She leans towards the view that the metrical part of The Paris Psalter had an Anglian original, citing H. Bartlett, The Metrical Division of The Paris Psalter (Baltimore: 1896), and R. Vleeskruyer, ed., The Life of St. Chad (Amsterdam: 1953) as authorities, and quotes from the latter: "the poetic part of the Paris Psalter certainly derives from an Anglian original", p.53. For a more complete study of these forms in V, see Richard Jordan's Eigentümlichkeiten des anglischen Wortschatzes (Heidelberg: 1906) on feogan/hatian, p.88: seað/pytt, pp.97-98: gewinn, p.43, note 2: wisdom, p.91: sehðe, pp.40-41: arwunga, p.59: selesgesceot, p.62: æfentid, p.117: and a chart on p.63 which includes the metrical part of P.

7. K. Sisam, "Dialect Origins in the Earlier Old English Verse", in Sisam, Studies in the History of Old English Literature (Oxford: 1953), p.121.

8. Ibid., p.126.

9. begun by Sisam's review of R. J. Menner, ed., The Poetical Dialogue of Solomon and Saturn (New York: 1941), in Medium Ævum 13 (1944), p.31ff.

10. Sisam, "Dialect Origins of the Earlier Old English Verse", p.138.

11. N. R. Ker, _A Catalogue of Manuscripts containing Anglo-Saxon_ (Oxford: 1957), item 338, p.412.

12. _Ibid._, item 49, p.82.

13. James Ure, ed., _The Benedictine Office_, p.25.

14. Max För̈ster, "Die altenglischen Texte der Pariser National-Bibliotek", _Englische Studien_ 62 (1927), p.130.

15. We must here note that both the mid-twelth-century interlinear glossed psalter designated E (Trinity College, Cambridge MS R. 17.i, edited as _Eadwine's Canterbury Psalter_ by Harsley and by Liles), and the BL MS Cotton Tiberius B.i poem _Menologium_ (whose date of composition is debateable) preserve quotations from V. Therefore copies of V must have been available throughout the south of England by 1150.

16. so noted by Colgrave, _The Paris Psalter_ (_E.E.M.F._ 8: 1958), p.17.

17. for D as a copy, cf. Sisam, _The Salisbury Psalter_, p.54.

18. cf. page 33 of this dissertation.

19. One would gain this impression of Æthelwold from Ælfric's "Life of St. Ethelwold" (MS Paris, latinus 5362): cf. Michael Winterbottom, ed., _Three Lives of English Saints_ (Toronto: 1972), esp. section 19, p.25.

20. Morrell, _A Manual of Old English Biblical Materials_, p.147.

Appendix

The following is a typescript of the text of the psalms and psalm-fragments from the Old English metrical Psalter used in this study. I have used the editions of Krapp and Dobbie in the <u>Anglo-Saxon</u> <u>Poetic</u> <u>Records</u>, volumes V and VI, and have underlined the words in each verse which appear in Collation Lists 1 through 4XY as entries for vocabulary comparison.

Psalm-fragments from Junius 121, Vj (Dobbie, pp. 80-83)

5:1 Word þu min onfoh,   wuldres ealdor
     and mid earum gehyr,   ece drihten.
     Ongyt mine clypunga   cuðum gereorde,
     beheald min gebed   holdum mode;
     þu eart min cyning   and eac ece god.

5:2 Forðon ic to ðe,   ece drihten,
     soðum gebidde,   and ðu symble gehyr
     morgena gehwylce   mine stefne.

5:3 Ic þe æt stande   ær on morgen
     and ðe sylfne geseo: forðon ic to soðe wat
     þæt ðu unriht ne wilt   ænig, drihten.

19:9 Do, drihten, cyng   dædum halne,
     and us eac gehyr   holdum mode,
     swylce we ðe daga,   drihten, cigen.

24:3 Do me wegas þine   wise, drihten,
     and me ðinra stiga   stapas eac gelær.

24:4 Gerece me on ræde   and me ricene gelær,
     þæt ic on þinre soðfæstnysse   simble lyfige.

24:5 Wes ðu gemyndig   miltsa þinra,
     þe ðu, drihten, dydest   syððan dagas wæron,
     and ðu wislice   þas woruld gesettest.

24:6 Ne gemynega þu me   minra fyrena
     gramra to georne,   þe ic geong dyde
     and me uncuðe   æghwær wæron;
     for ðinre þære myclan   mildheortnysse
     weorð gemyndig min,   mihtig drihten.

27:10 Hal do þin folc,   halig drihten,
      and ðin yrfe eac   eal gebletsa;
      rece þu heo swylce   and on riht ahefe,
      þæt hi on worulde   wynnum lifigen.

32:18 Wese þin mildheortnyse, mihtig drihten,
      wel ofer us,   swa we wenað on ðe.

34:1 Dem, drihten, nu   þa me deredon ær,
     afeoht swylce   þa me fuhtan to.

165

34:2   Gegrip gar and scyld,   and me georne gestand
       on fultume   wið feonda gryre.

34:3   Heald me herewæpnum   wið unholdum
       and wige beluc   wraðum feondum
       þe me ehtend   ealle syndon:
       sæge þonne syððan   sawle minre
       þæt ðu hire on hæle   hold gestode.

40:4   Ic nu mægene cweðe: "Miltsa me, drihten,
       hæl mine sawle,   forðon me hreoweð nu
       þæt ic firene on ðe   fremede geneahhige."

43:27 Aris, drihten, nu   and us ricene do
       fælne fultum,   and us æt feondum ahrede,
       forðon we naman þinne   nyde lufiað.

50:1   Mildsa me, mihtig drihten,   swa ðu manegum dydest,
       æfter ðinre þære mycelan   mildheortnysse.

50:10 Awend þine ansyne   a fram minum
       fræcnum fyrenum,   and nu forð heonon
       eall min unriht adwæsc   æghwær symle.

50:11 Syle me, halig god,   heortan clæne,
       and rihtne gast,   god, geniwa
       on minre gehigde   huru, min drihten.

50:12 Ne awyrp þu me,   wuldres ealdor,
       fram ðinre ansyne   æfre to feore,
       ne huru on weg aber   þone halgan gast,
       þæt he me færinga   fremde wyrðe.

50:13 Syle me þinre hælu   holde blisse,
       and me ealdorlice   æþele gaste
       on ðinne willan getryme,   weroda drihten.

Psalms from Paris MS Fonds latin 8824, Vp (Krapp, pp.3-29)

51:6   fore ænigre   egesan næfde,
       ne him fultum þær   fæstne gelyfde:
       ac he on his welan spede   wræste getruwode,
       and on idel gylp   ealra geornost.

51:7   Ic þonne swa elebeam   up weaxende
        on godes huse   ece gewene,
        and on milde mod   mines drihtnes,
        and me þæt to worulde   wat to helpe.

51:8   Ic þe andette   awa to feore
        on þære worulde   ðe þu geworhtest her:
        forðan þu eart se gooda,   gleaw on gesyhðe,
        þe þinne held curan,   þara haligra.

52:1   On his heortan cwæð   unhydig sum,
        ungleawlice,   þætte god nære;
        heo onsceoniendlice   syndon gewordene
        and heora willan   wraðe besmitene.

52:2   Næs þa goddoend   se þe god wiste,
        ne an furðum   ealra wære.

52:3   Þa of heofenum beseah   halig drihten
        ofer manna bearn,   hwæðer his mihta ða
        andgyt ænig   ealra hæfde,
        oððe god wolde   georne secan.

52:4   Ealle heo on ane   idelnesse
        symle besegan;   þa wæs soð nan mann
        þe god wolde   georne wyrcan;
        ne an furðum   ealra wære.

52:5   Ac ge þæs ealle ne magon   andgyt habban
        þe unrihtes   elne wyrceað
        and min folc fretað   swa fælne hlaf,
        ne hio god wyllað   georne ciegan;
        þær hio forhtigað,   frecnes egesan
        æniges ne þurfon.

52:6   Forþam manna ban   mihtig drihten
        liste tosceadeð,   þa him liciað;
        beoð þa gehyrwede   þe forhycggeað god.

52:7   Hwylc Isræla   ece hælu
        syleð of Sione   nymðe sylfa god,
        þonne he his folc   fægere alyseð
        of hæftnyde,   halig drihten?

52:8   Þonne Iacob byð   on glædum sælum
        and Isrælas   ealle bliðe.

53:1 On þinum þam haligan naman,   gedo me halne, god;
     alys me fram laðum   þurh þin leofe mægen.

53:2 God, min gebed   gearuwe gehyre,
     and earum onfoh   min agen word.

53:3 Forþam me fremde oft   facne gestodon,
     sohtan mine sawle   swiðe strange,
     and na heom god setton   gleawne on gesyhðe.

53:4 Efne me þonne god   gleawe fultumeð,
     is andfengea   ece drihten
     sawle minre;   he me swican ne wile.

53:5 Afyr me fæcne yfel   feonda minra,
     and hi soðfæst toweorp   syððan wide.

53:6 Ic ðe lustum   lace cweme,
     and naman þinne   niode swylce
     geara andette,   forðon ic hine goodne wat.

53:7 Forþon þu me alysdest,   lifes ealdor,
     of earfoðum   eallum symble,
     ealle mine fynd   eagum ofersawe.

54:1 Gehyr min gebed,   halig drihten,
     ne forseoh æfre   sariges bene;
     beheald me holdlice   and gehyr me eac.

54:2 Grimme ic eom begangen;   forðon ic gnornige
     and me forhtige   feondes stefne
     and fyrenfulra   fæcne niðas.

54:3 Forðam me on sah   unrihtes feala;
     wurdon me þa on yrre   yfele and hefige.

54:4 Ys me on hreðre heah   heorte gedrefed
     and me fealleð on   fyrhtu deaðes.

54:5 Egsa me and fyrhtu   ealne forcwomon,
     and me beþeahton   þeostru niðgrim.

54:6 Ic þa on mode cwæð,   hwa me sealde
     to fleogenne   fiðeru swa culfran,
     and ic þonne ricene   reste syððan.

54:7   Efne ic feor gewite,   fleame dæle,
       and on westene   wunode lange,
       bide þæs beornes   þe me bete eft
       modes mindom   and mægenes hreoh.

54:8   Hat nu todælan,   drihten usser,
       heora geðeode   geond þas woruld wide;
       forðon ic þær on unriht   oft locade,
       and wiðercwyda   wearn gehyrde;
       drugon þæt on burgum   dæges and nihtes.

54:9   Þunie him gewinnes wearn   ofer wealles hrof
       and heom on midle wese   man and inwit
       and unsoðfæstnys   ealle wealde.

54:10 Næfre on his weorþige   wea aspringe,
       mearce mansceat,   man inwides;
       forþon gif me min feond   fæcne wyrgeð,
       ic þæt abere   bliðe mode.

54:11 Þeah þe þa ealle   ðe me a feodon,
       wordum wyrigen   and wearn sprecan,
       ic me wið heora hete   hyde sneome.

54:12 Þu eart se man   þe me wære
       on anmede,   and æghwæs cuð
       latteow lustum;   and wyt gelome eac
       æton swetne mete   samed ætgædere,
       and on godes huse   gangan swylce
       mid geþeahtunge   þine and mine.

54:13 Hi ofer cume   unþinged deað,
       astigon heo on helle   heonan lifigende.

54:14 Forðam on heora gasthusum   is gramlic inwit,
       and on hiora midle   man inwitstæf.

54:15 Ic soðlice   to sylfum drihtne
       cleopode on corðre, and me cuðlice
       gehyrde   hælend drihten.

54:16 Ic on æfenne,   eac on mergenne
       and on midne dæg,   mægene sæcge
       and bodie,   þæt þu bliðe me
       mine stefne   stiðe gehyre.

54:17   A ðu symle   sawle mine
        lustum alyse, laðum wiðferige,
        forðon me manige ymb   mægene syrewað.

54:18   Þæt gehyreð god   and hi gehyneð eac,
        þe ær worulde wæs   and nu wunað ece.

54:19   Nis him onwendednes   on woruldlife,
        ne him godes fyrhtu   georne ondrædað.
        Heo besmitað   swylce his sylfes
        þa gewitnesse, þær hi woh fremedon;
        forðon hi synt on yrre   ut adælde,
        ne hi sylfe wel   geseon æfre,
        forðon hit wæs his heortan   gehygde neah.

54:20   Hi word hira   wel gesmyredon
        ele anlicast;   eft gewurdon
        on gescotfeohta   scearpe garas.

54:21   Sete on drihten   þin soð gehygð;
        he þe butan fracoðum   fedeð syððan.

54:22   Ne syleð he soðfæstum   syddan to feore
        þæt him yþende mod   innan hreðre;
        ðu arlease   ealle gelædest
        on soðe forwyrd   seaðes deopes.

54:23   Se blodhreowa wer   bealuinwites
        fæcne gefylled   ne fæger lif
        on middum feore   gemeteð ahwær;
        ic me on minne drihten   deorne getreowige.

55:1   Miltsa me drihten,   forðon me man tredeð,
        and me ealne dæg   mid unrihte
        fynd onfeohtað   þurh facensearu.

55:2   And me fæcne tredað   feondas mine,
        doð þæt ealne dæg   fram ærmergene.

55:3   Forðon monige synd   ðe to me feotað;
        wene ic me wraðe to ðe,   wuldres drihten.

55:4   Ic wealdend god   wordum herige
        and on god swylce   georne gelyfe,
        þæt minre spræce   sped folgie
        æghwæs ealne dæg;   eac ic swylce
        on god drihten   gearewe gewene;
        nis me ege mannes   for ahwæðer.

55:5   Hwæt, me ealne dæg   mine agen word
       sylfne socon, swyþe oncuðon,
       and wiðer me   wæran georne
       on yfel heora geðeaht   ealle onwende.

55:6   On eardiað,   þa ðe swa þenceað
       þæt heo gehyden   hælun mine,
       swa mine sawl bad   þæt ðu swylce heo
       for nahwæðer   nowiht hæle;
       on yrre þu folc   eall geðreatast.

55:7   Ic nu leofum gode   lif min secge,
       sette on ðinre gesyhðe   sarige tearas,
       swa ic ðe on gehate   hæfde geneahhige.

55:8   Þonne on hinderling   hweorfað mine
       feondas fæcne,   ðonne ic me freoðu to ðe
       wordum wilnige;   ic wat and can,
       þæt þu min god   gleawe wære.

55:9   Ic on god min word   georne herige,
       and on god swylce   georne gelyfe,
       and ic ealne dæg   ecne drihten
       wordum weorðige;   ne me wiht an siteð
       egesan awiht   æniges mannes.

55:10 On me synd, mihtig god,   þæt ic þe min gehat
       on herenesse   hyldo gylde;
       forþon ðu mine sawle   of swyltðeaðes
       laþum wiðlæddest, dydest lof stunde,
       aweredest mine eagan   wraðum tearum
       and min fet   fæle beweredest
       þæt ic gearewe   gode licode
       on lifigendra   leohte eallum.

56:1   Miltsa min, god,   and me milde weorð,
       forþon min sawel on þe   swyðe getryweð,
       and ic on fægerum scuan   fiðera ðinra
       gewicie,   oðþæt gewite forð
       and unriht me   eall beglide.

56:2   Heonan ic cleopige   to heahgode
       and to wealdendgode   ðe me wel dyde

56:3   He þa of heofenum   hider onsende
       þe me alysde,   laþum wiðferede,
       sealde on edwit   þe me ær trædan.

56:4   Sende mihtig god   his milde gehigd
       and his soðfæst mod   samoð ætgædere,
       and mine sawle   sona alysde
       of leon hwelpum   reðe gemanan;
       wæs ic slæpende   sare gedrefed.

56:5   Synd me manna bearn   mihtigum toðum
       wæpenstrælas   þa me wundedon;
       wæron hyra tungan getale   teonan gehwylcre
       and to yfele gehwam   ungemet scearpe.

56:6   Ahefe þe ofer heofenas,   halig drihten;
       is wuldur ðin   wide and side
       ofer ðas eorþan   ealle mære.

56:7   Fotum heo minum   fæcne grine
       grame gearwodon,   and geornlice
       mine sawle   swyðe onbigdon.

56:8   Hi deopne seað   dulfon widne
       þær ic eagum   on locade,
       and hi on ðone ylcan   eft gefeollan.

56:9   Gearo is min heorte   þæt ic gode cweme;
       gearo is min heorte   þæt ic gode swylce
       sealmas singe,   soðword sprece.

56:10 Aris, wuldur min, wynpsalterium,
       and ic on ærmergene   eac arise
       and min hearpe   herige drihten.

56:11 Ic þe on folcum   frine drihten
       ecne andete,   eac geond þeode
       sealmas singe   swiðe geneahhige.

56:12 Forðon þin mildheortnes   is mycel wið heofenas,
       is ðin soðfæstnes   swylce wið wolcnum.

56:13 Ahafen þu eart ofer heofenas,   halig drihten;
       is ofer ealle   eorðan swylce
       þines wuldres wlite   wide and side.

57:1   Gif ge soð sprecan   symble wyllen,
       demað manna bearn   domum rihtum.

57:2   Eft ge on heortan   hogedon inwit,
       worhton wraðe;   forþan ðæs wite eft
       on eowre handa   hefige geeode.

57:3   Ge firenfulle   fremde wurdon,
       syððan hi on worlde   wæron acende
       and heo on life   lygeword spæcon.

57:4   Yrre heom becume   anlic nædran
       ða aspide   ylde nemnað;
       seo hi deafe deð,   dytteð hyre earan,
       þæt heo nele gehyran   heahgaldor sum
       þæt snotre men   singað wið attrum.

57:5   God heora toðas   grame gescæned,
       þa hi on muðe   mycle habbað;
       tolyseð leona mægen   lungre drihten.

57:6   Ac hi forweorðan   wætere gelicost,
       þonne hit yrnende   eorðe forswelgeð;
       swa his bogan bendeð   oðþæt bitere eft
       adl on seteð,   swa his geearnuncg byð.

57:7   Swa weax melteð   gif hit byð wearmum neah
       fyre gefæstnad,   swa heo feallað on þæt
       hi sunnan ne geseoð   syððan æfre.

57:8   Ærðon eowre treowu   telgum blowe
       wæstmum weaxe,   ær him wol becimeð,
       þæt heo beoð on yrre   ealle forswelgene.

57:9   Soðfæst blissað,   þonne he sið ongan,
       hu þa arleasan   ealle forweorðað,
       and his handa ðwehð   on hæþenra
       and þæra fyrenfulra   fæcnum blode.

57:10 And þonne man cweþeð   on his modsefan:
       "Þis is wæstm   wises and goodes,
       þe his soðfæst weorc   symble læste."
       hi on eorðan god   ealle gedemeð.

58:11 Ahrede me, halig god,   hefiges niðes
       feonda minra,   ðe me feohtað to:
       alys me fram laðum   þe me lungre on
       risan willað,   nymðe þu me ræd geofe.

58:2   Genere me fram niþe   nahtfremmendra
       þe her unrihtes   ealle wyrceað,
       and me wið blodhreowes weres   bealuwe gehæle.

58:3 Þi nu mine sawle   swiþe bysige
      feondas mine   fæcne ofþryhtun,
      and me strange eac   stundum ongunnon;
      ne me unrihtes on   awiht wistan,
      ne ic firene eac   fremde drihtne.

58:4 Gif ic on unriht bearn   ic þæs eft geswac;
      on minne geanryne,   aris ðu, drihten, nu,
      and ðu sylfa gesyhst,   þæt ic swa dyde;
      þu eart mægena god,   mihtig drihten,
      and Isræla god   æghwær æt þearfe.

58:5 Beheald holdlice,   hu þu hraðe wylle
      geneosian   niða bearna
      ealra ðeoda   æghwær landes;
      ne þu hweðere on mode   milde weorðest
      eallum ðe unriht   elne wyrceað.

58:6 Hi æt æfene eft   in gecyrrað,
      þonne hy heardne   hungor þoliað,
      swa hundas ymbgað   hwommas ceastre.

58:7 Efne hi habbað on muðe   milde spræce,
      is him on welerum   wrað sweord and scearp,

58:8 Þonne gehyreð hwylc,   hwæt hyra hyge seceð?
      And ðu hi, drihten, dest   deope to bysmre:
      nafast þu for awiht   ealle þeoda.

58:9 Ic mine strengð on ðe   strange gehealde,
      forðon þu me god eart   geara andfencgea,
      and mildheortnes   mines drihtnes
      me fægere becom,   þær me wæs freondes þearf.

58:10 Min se goda god, ætyw me   þin agen good
      for minum feondum,   þe me feale syndun;
      ne do hy to deadan,   þy læs hi dollice
      þinre æ geban   anforlæton.

58:11 Ac þu hi wide todrif   þurh þines wordes mægen
      and hi wraðe toweorp   wealdend min drihten.

58:12 Ys hyra muðes scyld   manworda feala,
      ða hi mid welerum   wraðe aspræcan;
      wærun hi on oferhygde   ealle gescende,
      þa hi on lige   lange feredon;
      forðon hi on ende   yrre forgripeð
      and hi syþþan ne boeð   samod ætgædere.

58:13   Syððan hi wisslice witon,   þætte wealdeð god
        ofer middangeard   manna cynnes
        and ealra eac   eorðan gemæru.

58:14   Hi on æfenne   eft gecyrrað
        and heardne eac   hungor ðoliað,
        swa hundas ymbað   hwommas ceastre.

58:15   Efne hi to æte   ut gewitað,
        þær hi towrecene   wide hweorfað;
        gif hi fulle ne beoð,   fela gnorniað.

58:16   Ic þonne ðine strengþu   stundum singe
        and ðin milde mod   morgena gehwylce.

58:17   Forðon þu min andfengea   æghwær wære
        and ic helpe æt ðe   hæfde symble,
        þonne me costunge   cnysedon geneahhige;
        þu eart fultum min,   ic ðe fela singe.

58:18   Forðon þu me, god, eart   geara andfengea
        and mildheortnes,   mihtig drihten.

59:1   Þu us todrife,   drihten user,
        and us towurpe   geond werþeoda,
        yrre us wurde   and eft milde.

59:2   Eorðan ðu onhrerdest,   ealle gedrefdest;
        hæl hyre wunde,   nu heo ahrered is.

59:3   Feal ðu ætywdest   folce ðinum
        heardra wisan   and hi hraþe æfter
        mid wynsume   wine drenctest.

59:4   Þu becnuncge   beorhte sealdest,
        þam þe ege ðinne   elne healdað,
        þæt hi him gebeorgen   bogan and stræle
        and wæron alysde   leofe þine.

59:5   Do me þin seo swyðre hand   symle halne;
        gehyr me, halig god.   Hwæt, ðu holdlice
        on ðinre halignesse   her aspræce:
        "And ic blissie ba gedæle
        Sicimam et Convallem, ða samod wæron
        on Metiboris   mihtum spedige,

59:6   Min is Galaad,   gleaw Mannases
       and Effrem ys   æðele strengþu
       heafdes mines   her on foldan.

59:7   Cyninc ys me   Iuda cuð;
       is me Moab   mines hyhtes hwer,
       and ic aðenige eac   on Idumea,
       min gescy sende,   and me syððan gedo
       Allophilas   ealle gewylde."

59:8   Hwylc gelædeð me   leofran on ceastre
       weallum beworhte?   Hwa wyle swylce me
       in Idumea   eac gelædan?

59:9   Ac ne eart þu se sylfa god,   ðe us swa drife?
       Ne ga ðu us on mægene,   mihtig drihten.

59:10 Syle us nu on earfoðum   æðelne fultum,
       forðon hælu byð   her on eorðan
       manna gehwylces   mægenes idel.

59:11 Us sceal mægenes gemet   mihtig drihten
       soðfæst syllan,   and he sona mæg
       ure fynd gedon   fracoþe to nahte.

60:1   Gehyr, halig god,   hraþe mine bene,
       beheald mine gebed   holde mode.
       Nu ic of eorðan   utgemærum
       cleopige to þe   nu me caru beateð
       heard æt heortan,   help min nu þa;
       ahefe me holdlice   on halne stan.

60:2   Þu me gelæddest   mid lufan hyhte,
       wære me se stranga tor   stið wið feondum.

60:3   Ic eardige   awa to feore
       on ðinum selesgesceote;   þær me softe byð,
       þær ic beo fægere beþeaht   fiðerum ðinum.

60:4   Forðon ðu gehyrdest,   halig drihten
       hu min gebed to ðe   beorhte eode;
       yrfe þu sealdest   anra gehwylcum,
       se þe naman ðinne   þurh neod forhtað.

60:5   Dæg byð ofer dæge,   þær byð gedefe cynincg
       beoð his winter eac   wynnum iced,
       oð þone dæg þe he   on drihtnes sceal

176

on ansyne　andweard gangan,
and þær to worlde　wunian ece.

60:6　Hwylc seceð þæt　þe soðfæst byð?
Swa ic naman ðinum　neode singe,
þæt ic min gehat　her agylde
of dæge on dæg,　swa hit gedefe wese.

61:1　Ic mine sawle　symble wylle
full gleawlice　gode underþeodan;
æt him is hælu min　her eall gelancg.

61:2　Hwæt, he is god min　and gearu hælend;
is he fultum min,　ic ne forhtige wiht.

61:3　Ðonne ge mid mane　men ongunnon,
ealle ge ða to deadan　dædun sona,
swa ge awurpon　wah of stofne.

61:4　Swa ge mine are　ealle þohton
wraðe toweorpan,　wide urnon
þurstige muðe;　þæne bletsadan
and ðone wyrgedan　wraðe mid heortan.

61:5　Hwæðere ic me soðe　sawle mine
to gode hæfde　georne geðeoded;
he minre geðylde　þingum wealdeð.

61:6　Hwæt, he is god min　and gleaw hælend
and fultum is;　ne mæg ic on hine ahwær befleon.

61:7　On gode standeð　min gearu hælu
and wuldor min　and wyn mycel;
me is halig hyht　on hine swylce.

61:8　Hycge him halig folc　hælu to drihtne;
doð eowre heortan hige　hale and clæne,
forðon eow god standeð　georne on fultum.

61:9　Hwæðere ge, manna bearn,　manes unlyt
wyrceað on wægum　and woh doð,
and eow beswicað　sylfe oftast,
þær ge idel gylp　on þam ilcan fremmað.

61:10　Nellað ge gewenan　welan unrihte
oþþe to reaflace　ræda þencean.

177

61:11 Þeah þe eow wealan to   wearnum flowen,
       nyllan ge eow on heortan þa   hige staðelian;
       æne ic god spræcan   gearuwe gehyrde
       and þæt treowe ongeat   tidum gemeldad.

61:12 Miht is drihtnes   ofer middangeard
       and him þæs to worlde   wuldor stande
       and mildheortness,   þæt he manna gehwam
       æfter his agenum   earnungum demeð,
       efne swa he wyrceð   on worldlife.

62:1   God min, god min,   ic þe gearuwe to
       æt leohte gehwam   lustum wacie.

62:2   Min sawl on ðe   swyðe   byrsteð
       and min flæsc on ðe   fæste getreoweð.

62:3   On westene   and on wege swylce
       and on wæterflodum   wene ic swiðe,
       þæt ic ðe on halgum   her ætywe,
       þæt ic þin wuldur and mægen   wis sceawige

62:4   Ys þin milde mod   and micele betere
       þonne þis læne lif   þe we lifiað on;
       weleras ðe mine   wynnum heriað.

62:5   Swa ic ðe on minum life   lustum bletsige
       and ic on naman þinum   neode swylce
       mine handa þwea   halgum gelome.

62:6   Ys sawl min   swetes gefylled,
       swa seo fætte gelynd   fægeres smeoruwes;
       weleras mine   wynnum swylce
       þinne naman nu ða   neode heriað.

62:7   Swa ic þin gemynd   on modsefan
       on minre reste   rihte begange,
       and on ærmergen on ðe   eac gewene,
       forðon þu me on fultum   fæste gestode.

62:8   Ic beo fægere beþeaht   fiðerum þinum
       and hiht on ðon   hæbbe georne
       forðon min sawl on ðe   soðe getreoweþ:
       me ðin seo swiðre onfencg   symble æt ðearfe.

62:9   Forðon hi on idel   ealle syððan
       sohton synlice   sawle mine,
       and geond eorðscræfu   eodon geneahhe;
       nu hi wæran geseald   under sweordes hand,
       syndon fracuðe nu   foxes dælas.

62:10 Kynincg sceal on drihtne   clæne blisse
       hluttre habban,   and hine heriað eac
       ealle þa ðe on hine   aðas sweriað;
       forþon synt gemyrde   muðas ealle
       þa unriht sprecað   ahwær landes.

63:1   Gehyr min gebed,   halig drihten,
       nu me costunge   cnyssað geneahhe,
       and wið egesan   yfeles feondes
       mine sawle gescyld   symle æt þearfe.

63:2   Þu me oft aweredest   wyrigra gemotes
       and fram þære menegeo   þe man woldon
       and unrihte   æghwær fremman.

63:3   Þa heora tungan teoð   teonan gehwylce
       sweorde efenscearpe   and heora swiðne bogan
       and unscyldige mid þy   scotian þenceað.

63:4   Hi hine samnuncga   scearpum strelum
       on scotiað,   egsan ne habbað,
       ac hi mid wraðum   wordum trymmað
       and sare sprecað: Hwa gesyhð usic?

63:5   Swa hi smeagað oft   swiðost unriht
       and on þam ilcan   eft forweorðað,
       þær hi mamriað   man and unriht.

63:6   Gangeð man manig   modig on heortan,
       oðþæt hine ahefeð   hælend drihten.

63:7   Syndon hyra wita   scytelum cilda
       æghwæs onlicost: ne him awiht þon ma
       heora tungan nu   teonan on sittað.

63:8   Ealle synd gedrefede   þe hi on sioð;
       sceal him manna gehwylc   man ondrædan
       and weorc godes   wide mærsian
       and his weorc ongitan   mid wisdome.

63:9   Se soðfæsta   symble on drihten
       blissað baldlice,   bote gewened,
       and hine heriað eac   heortan clæne.

64:1   Þe gedafenað   drihten user,
       þæt þe man on Sion   swyðe herige
       and on Hierusalem   gylde and gehate.

64:2   Gehyr min gebed,   halig drihten,
       for ðe sceal ælc flæsc   forð siðian.

64:3   Synfulra word   swyþe ofer usic
       fræcne foran: þu gefultuma
       urum misdædum,   mihta wealdend.

64:4   He weorðeð eadig   se þe hine ece god
       cystum geceoseð   and hine clæne hafað,
       and on his earduncgstowum   eardað syððan.

64:5   Ealle we ðin hus   ecum godum
       fægere fyllað;   fæste is þin templ
       ece and wræclic   awa to feore.

64:6   Gehyr us, hælend god,   þu eart hyht ealra
       þe on ðysse eorðan   utan syndon
       oþþe feor on sæ   foldum wuniað.

64:7   Þinre mihte sculon   muntas hyran
       swylce þu gedrefest   deope wælas
       þæt byð ormætum   yþa hlude
       and hi uneaðe mæg   ænig aræfnan.

64:8   Þeoda him ondrædað   þinne egesan,
       þe eard nymað   utan landes;
       for þinum wundrum   forhte weorðað.

64:9   Ærmorgenes gancg   wið æfentid
       ealle þa deman   drihten healdeð;
       eorðan ðu gefyllest   eceum wæstmum,
       þæt heo welig weorþeð   wera cneorissum.

64:10 Beoð godes streamas   gode wætere
       fæste gefylde,   þanan feorhnere
       findað foldbuend,   swa him fægere oft
       gegearewadest,   god lifigende.

64:11 Wæter yrnende   wæstme tyddrað:
      mænige on moldan   manna cynnes
      on cneorisse   cende weorðað,
      and blissiað   blowað and growað
      þurh dropunge   deawes and renes.

64:12 Þonne þu geares hring   mid gyfe bletsast
      and þine fremsumnesse wylt   folcum dælan,
      þonne beoð þine feldas   fylde mid wæstmum.

64:13 Þonne on wæstmum   weorðað mæsted,
      and mid wynngrafe   weaxeð geswiru.

64:14 Hi beoð gegyrede   godre wulle,
      eowdesceapum: cumað eadilic
      wæstm on wangas   weorðlic on hwætum;
      þonne hi cynlice to ðe   cleopiað sona,
      and þe þonne lustum   lofe þanciað.

65:1 Ealle eorðbuend   ecne drihten
      wordum wislicum   wide herian,
      and his naman secgeað   neode mid sealmum
      and him wuldres lof   wide syllað.

65:2 And gode secgeað,   hu his þa goodan weorc
      syndon wundorlice   wide geond eorðan,
      and eac on menigeo   mægenes þines
      þine feondas þe   fæcne leogað.

65:3 Geweorðie   wuldres ealdor
      eall ðeos eorþe,   ecne drihten;
      and þe singe eac,   secge geneahhie,
      þæt þin nama is   ofer eall niða bearn
      se hehsta   hæleþa cynnes.

65:4 Cumað nu and geseoð,   hu cyme weorc
      drihten worhte;   synt his domas eac
      swiþe egeslice   ofer eall ylda bearn.

65:5 He mæg onwendan   wætera ðryðe,
      þæt þas deopan sæ   drige weorðað,
      and þa strangan mæg   streamas swylce
      gefeterian,   þæt þu mid fote miht
      on treddian   eorðan gelice.

65:6 He mægen wealdeð   ofer eall manna cyn
      on ecnesse   awa to feore,

and he ofer ealle þeode eagum wliteð;
þa hine on yrre æghwær gebringað,
ne beoð þa on him sylfum syððan ahafene.

65:7 Bletsigen þeoda bliðe mode
ealle eorðbuend ecne drihten
and mid stefne lof strang asecgean.

65:8 He mine sawle sette to life
ne læteð mine fet laðe hreran.

65:9 Ure costade god clæne fyre
soðe dome, swa man seolfor deð,
þonne man hit aseoðeð swyðe mid fyre.

65:10 Þu us on grame swylce gryne gelæddest,
and us bealuwa fela on bæce standeð;
settest us mænige eac men ofer heafod.

65:11 We þuruh fyr farað and þuruh floda þrym,
and ðu us on colnesse clæne gelæddest.

65:12 Ic on þin hus halig gange
and þær tidum þe tifer onsecge;
þær ic min gehat mid hyge gylde
þæt mine weleras ær wise gedældan.

65:13 Þas ic mid muðe aspræc mine æt þearfe,
þær me costunge cnyssedan geneahhe,
þæt ic ðe on tifrum teala forgulde
ealle þa gehat, þe ic æfre her
mid minum welerum wis todælde.

65:14 Gehyrað me and her cumað:
ic eow mid soþe secgean wylle,
gif ge godes egesan georne habbað,
hu mycel he dyde minre sawle.

65:15 Þuruh his mihte ic muðe cleopige
oþþe mine tungan tidum blissade.

65:16 Gif ic me unrihtes oncneow awiht on heortan,
ne wite me þæt wealdend drihten.

65:17 Forðon me gehyrde hælend drihten,
and minre stefne beheold strange bene.

65:18	Drihten si gebletsad, þe he ne dyde æfre nymðe he mine bene bealde gehyrde, ne his milde mod me dyde fremde.
66:1	Miltsa us, mihtig drihten, and us on mode eac gebletsa nu; beorhte leohte þinne andwlitan, and us on mode weorð þuruh þine mycelnesse milde and bliðe.
66:2	And we þæs on eorðan andgyt habbað, ure wegas wide geond þas werðeode on þinre hælo healdan motan.
66:3	Folc þe andette; þu eart fæle god, and þe andetten ealle þeoda.
66:4	Hæbbe þæs gefean folca æghwylc and blissien bealde þeoda, þæs þe þu hi on rihtum rædum demest and eorðbuende ealle healdest.
66:5	Folc þe andette fælne drihten and þe andetten ealle þeoda.
66:6	Ge him eorðe syleð æþele wæstme; gebletsige us bliðe drihten and user god eac bletsige; hæbbe his egesan eall eorþan gemæru.
67:1	Arise god, ricene weorðe his feonda gehwylc fæste toworpen: fleoð his ansyne, þa þe hine feodan ær.
67:2	Rece hi gelicast ricene geteoriað: swa fram fyre weax floweð and mylteð, swa þa fyrenfullan frecne forweorðað; habbað soðfæste symbel ece.
67:3	Hi ansyne ecean drihtnes habbað beorhtlice blisse and sibbe.
67:4	Singað soðum gode sealmas geneahhige, and his naman swylce neode heriað: doð siðfæt þæs seftne and rihtne, þe he sylfa astah ofer sunnan up, þam is to naman nemned drihten.

67:5 Wesað ge on his gesyhþe   symble bliðe,
     and on his ansyne wesan   ealle gedrefde,
     þa þe wydewum syn   wraðe æt dome
     oþþe steopcildum wesen   strange fæderas.

67:6 Drihten is on his stowe   dema halig,
     se þe eardian deð   anes modes
     and on hiora huse   healdeð blisse;

67:7 Se þe on his mængenes   mihte gelædeð
     þæt he þa gehæftan   hæleð sniome,
     and þe to yrre beoð   ealle gecigde
     and eardiað   on eorðscræfum.

67:8 Þonne god gangeð   for his þæt gleawe folc,
     oððe geond westena   wide feroð,
     þanon eorðe byð   eall onhrered.

67:9 For ansyne   ecean drihtnes
     heofenas droppetað;   hrusan forhtiað
     for Isræla godes   egesan þrymme.

67:10 Wilsumne regn   wolcen brincgeð,
      and þonne ascadeð god   sundoryfe;
      eall þu þa gefremest   þurh þine fæste miht.

67:11 Þine wihte on þam   wynnum lifiað:
      þu þin swete good   sealdest þearfum.

67:12 God gifeð gleaw word   godspellendum,
      syleð him modes mægen   se þe is mihtig kynincg
      and wlites wealdend;   oft weorðlic reaf
      on huse men   her gedælað.

67:13 Gif ge slæpað   samod on clero
      fiðeru beoþ culfran   fægeres seolfres
      and hire bæc scineð   beorhtan golde.

67:14 Þonne hi se heofonlica kynincg   her toscadeð,
      syþþan hi on Selmon   snawe weorðað.

67:15 Gebeorh godes   bringeð to genihte
      wæstme weorðlice   and wel þicce.

67:16 Forþon ge onfoð   fægerum beorge,
      þær ge to genihte   geniomað wæstme;
      se is wealdendgode   wel liciendlic,
      on þam wið ende   eardað drihten.

67:17　　Wærun godes cræta　　gegearwedra
　　　　 tyn þusendo　　geteled rime,
　　　　 mænigfeald þusend　　modblissiendra.

67:18　　Drihten is on þam　　dædum spedig;
　　　　 on heahnesse astah,　　hæftned lædde,
　　　　 þa on hæftnede　　hwile micele
　　　　 lange lifdon,　　and wæs lacgeofa.
　　　　 ofer middangeard　　manna bearnum.

67:19　　Ne magon þær eard niman　　ungeleafe menn;
　　　　 wese of dæge on dæg　　drihten user,
　　　　 se goda god,　　georne gebletsad.

67:20　　Sylle us gesundne　　siðfæt drihten;
　　　　 ure hælend god　　helpe usser
　　　　 and us æt deaðe eac　　drihten gehealde.

67:21　　Hwæðere wealdend god　　wiðhycgendra
　　　　 heafdas feonda　　her gescæneð,
　　　　 and he tofylleð　　feaxes scadan
　　　　 þara þe her on scyldum　　swærum eodon.

67:22　　Of Basan, cwæð　　bealde drihten,
　　　　 ic me on sæ deopre　　sniome onwende,
　　　　 oþþæt þin fot weorðe　　fæste on blode.

67:23　　Hundes tungan　　habbað feondas,
　　　　 from þam þine gangas　　wæron gesewene;
　　　　 wærun godes mines　　gangas rihte,
　　　　 soðes kynincges　　symble on halgum.

67:24　　Þyder ealdormen　　ofstum coman,
　　　　 and gegaderade　　gleowe sungon
　　　　 on þæra manna　　midle geongra
　　　　 on tympanis　　togenum strengum,
　　　　 and on ciricean　　Crist, drihten god
　　　　 bealde bletside　　bearn Isræla,

67:25　　Þæt Benniamines synt　　bearn on geogoðe
　　　　 and ealdormenn　　eac of Iudan,
　　　　 þe latteow wæs　　forð þara leoda,
　　　　 and ealdras eac　　of Zabulone
　　　　 and Neptalim　　niode swylce.

67:26　　Bebeod þinum mægene;　　þu eart mihtig god;
　　　　 and þin weorc on us　　mid wisdome
　　　　 getryme on þinum temple　　tidum gehalgod;
　　　　 þæt ys on Hierusalem,　　þyder ðe gyfe lædað
　　　　 of feorwegum　　foldan kynincgas.

67:27 On wuda þu wildeor   wordum þreatast
       and fearra gemot   under folcum:
       ne beoð ut fram þe   æfre atynde,
       þa þe seolfres beoð   since gecoste.

67:28 Toweorp þu þa ðeoda ..... (LACUNA)

68:1 Do me halne, god,   forþon hreoh wæter
     to minum feore inn   floweð and gangeð;
     eom ic on lame oflegd,   hafað lytle sped.

68:2 Com ic on sæs hricg,   þær me sealt wæter
     hreoh and hopig   holme besencte.

68:3 Þær ic werigmod   wann and cleopode,
     þæt me grame syndan   goman hase:
     byð me æt þam earon   eagon wiðgangen:
     hwæðere ic on god minne   gearewe gewene.

68:4 Hiora is mycle ma   þonne ic me hæbbe
     on heafde nu   hæra feaxes,
     þe me earwunga   ealle feogeað.

68:5 Ofer me syndon   þa þe me ehton,
     fæstum folmum   forð gestrangad
     feondas mine,   and ic forð agef
     unrihtlice   þa þe ic ne reafude ær.

68:6 Þu wast, wuldres god,   þæt ic eom unwis hyges,
     ne wæren þe bemiðene   mine scylde.

68:7 Ne sceolon æt me   ænige habban
     sceame sceandlice   þe þines siðes her
     ful bealdlice   biðað, drihten.
     Þu eart mægena god;   ne sceal æt me
     ænige unare   ahwær findan,
     þe ðe Isræla god   ahwær seceað.

68:8 Forþon ic edwit for þe   oft aræfnade
     and me hleorsceame   hearde becwoman,
     and ic framþe wearð   fæderenbroðrum,
     wæs unmæge gyst   modorcildum.

68:9 Forþon me þines huses   heard ellenwod
     æt ormæte   and me eac fela
     þinra edwita   on gefeollon.

68:10   Þonne ic minum feore   fæsten gesette,
        eall hi me þæt on edwit   eft oncyrdan.

68:11   Gif ic mine gewæda   on witehrægl
        cyme cyrde,   cwædan hi syþþan,
        þæt ic him wæfersyn   wære eallum.

68:12   Me wiðerwearde   wæron ealle,
        þa him sæton   sundor on portum:
        spræcon me wraðe,   þa þe win druncon.

68:13   Ic þonne min gebed   to þe, mihtig drihten,
        tidum sende   teala liciendlic,
        and þu me þonne on mænigeo   miltsa þinra
        gehyre me hlutre   hælu þine.

68:14   Alys me of lame,   þe læs ic weorþe lange fæst,
        and me feondum afyrr, frea ælmihtig:
        ado me of deope   deorces wæteres,
        þe læs me besencen   sealte flodas.

68:15   Ne me huru forswelge   sægrundes deop
        ne me se seað   supe mid muðe.

68:16   Gehyr, drihten, me   forþon gedefe is
        þin milde mod   mannum fremsum,
        and for mænigeo   miltsa þinra
        geseoh on me   swylce, drihten.

68:17   Ne acyr þu æfre fram þinum cnihte   þin clæne gesyhð,
        forþan me feondas to   feohtað geneahhe;
        gehyr me hrædlice   and me help freme.

68:18   Beheald mine sawle   and hi hrædlice
        alys and wiðfere   laþum feondum.

68:19   .. (LACUNA)

                          arscame;
        for þinre ansyne   ealle syndon
        þe feondas me   fæcne wurdon.

68:20   Min heorte gebad   hearmedwit feala
        and yrmðu mænig   eac aræfnede:
        næfde eorla þæs   ænig sorge;
        frefrend ic sohte,   findan ic ne mihte.

68:21   Hi minne mete   mengdan wið geallan
        and þa gedrugadne   drenctan mid ecede.

68:22   Wese heora beod fore him   wended on grine
        and on edlean yfel   and on æwisce.

68:23   Syn hiora eagan   eac adimmad,
        þæt hi geseon ne magon   syþþan awiht;
        weorðe heora bæc swylce   abeged eac.

68:24   Ageot ofer hi   þin þæt grame yrre,
        and æbylignes eac   yrres þines
        hi forgripe   gramhicgende.

68:25   Wese wic heora   weste and idel;
        ne on heora eðele ne sy   þinc oneardiendes.

68:26   Forþon hi ealra   ehtan ongunnon,
        ðe þu him earfoðu   ænig geafe,
        and me wean ecton   minra wunda sar.

68:27   Asete him þa unriht to   þe hi geearneda
        and mid unrihte   ær geworhton,
        and hi on þin soðfæst weorc   syþþan ne gangan.

68:28   Syn hi adilgad   of gedefra eac
        þæra lifigendra   leofra bocum;
        ne wesen hi mid soðfæstum   syþþan awritene.

68:29   Ic me sylfa eam   sarig þearfa,
        and me andwlita onfeng   ecean drihtnes,
        se me holdlice hælde sona.

68:30   Nu ic naman drihtnes   neode herige
        and hine mid lofsange   læde swylce.

68:31   Ic þam leofan gode   licie swyþor
        þonne æðele cealf,   þeah þe him upp aga
        horn on heafde   oððe hearde cleo.

68:32   Geseoð þæt and gefeoð,   sarie þearfan,
        seceað drihten   and eower sawl leofað.

68:33   Forþam þa þearfendan   þriste drihten
        gehyreð holdlice;   nyle he gehæfte eac
        on heora neode   na forhycgan.

68:34   Herige hine swylce   heofen and eorðe,
        side sæflodas   and þa him syndon on.

68:35   Forþon Sione god   symble hæleð;
        beoð mænige byrig   mid Iudeum
        eft getimbrade,   þær hi eard nimað.

68:36   Þær hi yrfestol   eft gesittað
        and hiora eþel begytað   esnas drihtenes,
        and his naman   neode lufiað,
        þær eardiað   awa to feore.

69:1   Wes, drihten god,   deore fultum;
        beheald, drigten, me,   and me hraðe syþþan
        gefultuma   æt feorhþearfe.

69:2   Þonne beoð gescende   and scame dreogað,
        þa þe mine fynd   fæcne wæron
        and mine sawle   sohton mid niðe.

69:3   Hi on hinderlincg   hweorfað and cyrrað;
        ealle hiora scamien,   þe me yfel hogedon.

69:4   And heora æfstu eac   ealle sceamien,
        þe me word cwædon: "Weg la, weg la!"

69:5   Habban þa mid wynne   weorðe blisse,
        þa þe secean   symble drihten,
        and symble cweðen: "Sy þin miht, drihten!"
        and þine hælu   holde lufigean.

69:6   Ic eom wædla   and worldþearfa;
        gefultuma me, god   frea ælmihtig.

69:7   Þu me fultum eart   fæste, drihten,
        eart alysend min;   ne lata þu awiht.

70:1   Ic on þe, god drihten,   gearuwe gewene:
        ne weorðe ic on ealdre   æfre gescended:
        þu me snione alys   þuruh þine þa swiþeran miht.

70:2   Ahyld me þin eare to   holde mode,
        and me lustum alys   and me lungre weorð
        on god drihten   georne þeccend
        and on trume stowe,   þæt þu me teala hæle.

70:3   Forþon þu me, god, wære   geara trymmend,
       freoða fultumiend;   alys me eondum nu,
       and me of folmum afere   firenwyrcendra,
       þe þine æ efnan nellað;
       syndon unrihtes   ealle wyrcende.

70:4   Forþon þu me eart fæle geþyld   fæste, drihten
       wære me on geoguðe hyht   gleaw æt frymðe.

70:5   Ic of modur hrife   mundbyrd on þe
       þriste hæfde; þu eart þeccend min;
       on þe ic singge nu   symble and geneahhie.

70:6   Ic eom swa forebeacen   folce manegum,
       and þu me eart fultum strang   fæste æt þearfe.

70:7   Sy min muð and min mod   mægene gefylled,
       þæt ic þin lof mæge   lustum singan
       and wuldur þin   wide mærsian
       and þe ealne dæg   æghwær herian.

70:8   Ne aweorp þu me,   wuldres ealdor,
       þonne me ylde tid   on gesige;
       þonne me mægen and mod   mylte on hreðre,
       ne forlæt þu me   lifigende god.

70:9   Oft me feala cwædon   feondas yfele,
       and sætendan   sawle minre
       and on anre geþeaht   eodan togædere.

70:10 Cweþað cuðlice: "Wuton cunnian,
       hwænne hine god læte   swa swa gymeleasne;
       þonne we hine forgripen   and his geara ehtan;
       syþþan he ne hæbbe   helpend ænne."

70:11 Ne ofgif þu me huru,   god ælmihtig;
       beseoh þu me, soð god,   symble on fultum.

70:12 Beoð gedrette,   eac gescende,
       þa mine sawle ær   swyþust tældun,
       byð þam scand and sceamu   þe me syrwedan yfel.

70:13 Ic me symble on god   swiðost getreowige,
       ofer eall þin lof   lengest hihte.

70:14 Min muð sægeð   þine mægenspede
       and þin soðfæst weorc   swyþust mæreð,
       sægeð þe ealne dæg   ece hælu.

70:15   Forþon ic ne ongeat   grame ceapunga,
        ac ic on þine þa myclan   mihte gange.

70:16   Ic þine soðfæstnesse geman   symble, dirhten;
        þu me ara, god,   ærest lærdest
        of geoguðhade;   nu ic eom gomel wintrum.
        A ic wundor þin   weorþlic sægde,
        and ic þæt wið oryldu   awa fremme;
        ne forlæt þu me,   lifigende god.

70:17   Oððæt ic þines earmes   eall asecge
        stiþe strencðe   þisse cneorisse,
        eallum þam teohhe,   þe nu toweard ys,

70:18   Þines mihtes þrym,   and þæt mære soð,
        þæt ðe on heofenum, god,   heah geworhtest
        wundur wræclicu;   nis þe, wuldres cyning,
        ænig æfre gelic,   ece drihten.

70:19   Oft þu me ætywdest   earfoðes feala
        on costunge   cuðra manna,
        and me yfela feala   oft oncnyssedest;
        þonne þu yrre þin   eft oncyrdest
        and me on neowelnesse eft   neoðan alysdest
        þysse eorðan,   þe we on buiað.

70:20   Ðær þy þin soðfæst weorc   sniome tobræddest,
        þonne þu gehwyrfdest   and hulpe min,
        and me getrymedest   þæt ic teala mihte;
        forþon ic þe andette,   ece drihten,
        and þe on sealmfatum   singe be hearpan,
        Isræla god,   ece and halig.

70:21   Mine weleras gefeoð,   wynnum lofiað,
        þonne ic þe singe,   sigora wealdend,
        and min sawl eac,   þa þu sylf lysdest.

70:22   Swylce min tunge   tidum mærde
        þin soðfæst weorc;   scende wæron ealle,
        þe me yfel to   ær gesohton.

Psalm-fragments from Vj (Dobbie, pp.84-85)

79:18   Gehweorf us, mægna god,   and us milde æteow,
        þinne andwlitan: ealle we beoð hale.

84:4   Gehweorf us hraðe,   hælend drihten,
       and ðin yrre fram us   eac oncyrre.

87:13 Ic me to ðe,   ece drihten,
       mid modgehygde   mægene clypede,
       and min gebed   morgena gehwylce
       fore sylfne ðe   soðfæst becume.

89:15 Gehweorf us hwæthwygu,   halig drihten;
       wes ðinum scealcum   wel eaðbene.

89:18 Geseoh þine scealcas   swæsum eagum,
       and on þin agen weorc,   ece drihten,
       and heora bearn gerece   bliðum mode.

89:19 Wese us beorhtnys ofer   bliðan drihtnes,
       ures þæs godan godes   georne ofer ealle;
       gerece ure handgeweorc   heah ofer usic.

Psalm-fragments Vp (Krapp, p.67)

94:1   Cumað nu togædere,   wutun cweman gode,
       wynnum drihten   wealdend herigean,
       urum hælende   hyldo gebeodan.

94:2   Wutun his ansyne   ærest secean,
       þæt we andettan   ure fyrene
       and we sealmas him   singan mid wynne.

94:3   Forðon is se micla god   mihtig drihten
       and se micla cynincg   ofer eall manna godu.

94:4   Forðon ne wiðdrifeð   drihten usser
       his agen folc   æfre æt þearfe;
       he þas heahbeorgas   healdeð swylce.

94:5   Eac he sæs wealdeð   and he sette þone;
       worhte his folme eac   foldan drige.

94:6   Cumað him fore   and cneow bigeað
       on ansyne   ures drihtnes,
       and him wepan fore   ðe us worhte ær.

94:7   Forðon he is drihten god,   dema usser;
       wærun we his fæle folc   and his fægere sceap,
       þa he on his edisce   ær afedde.

94:8   Gif ge to dæge   drihtnes stefne
       holde gehyran,   næfre ge heortan geþanc
       deorce forhyrden   drihtnes willan.

94:9   Swa on grimnesse   fyrn geara dydan
       on þam wraðan dæge   and on westenne,
       þær min ðurh facen   fæderas eowre
       þisse cneorisse   cunnedan georne,
       þær hi cunnedan   cuð ongeaton
       and min sylfes weorc   gesawon mid eagum.

94:10 Nu ic feorwertig   folce þyssum
       wintra rimes   wunade neah,
       aa and symble cwæð   and eac swa oncneow,
       þæt hi on heortan   hyge dysegedan.

94:11 Hi wegas mine   wihte ne oncneowan,
       þæt ic ær on yrre   aðe benemde,
       gif hi on mine reste   ricene eodon.

Psalm-fragments from Vj (Dobbie, pp.85-86)

101:1 Þu min gebed,   mære drihten,
       gehyr, heofenes weard,   and gehlyde min
       to ðe becume,   þeoda reccend.

102:1 Bletsa, mine sawle,   bliðe drihten,
       and eall min inneran   his þone ecan naman.

102:2 Bletsige, mine sawle,   bealde drihten,
       ne wilt ðu ofergeotul   æfre weorðan
       ealra goda   þe he ðe ær dyde.

102:3 He þinum mandædum   miltsade eallum
       and ðine adle   ealle gehælde.

102:4 Se alysde þin lif   leof of forwyrde,
       fylde þinne willan   fægere mid gode.

102:5   He ðe gesigefæste   soðre mildse
        and ðe mildheorte   mode getrymede;
        eart ðu edniwe   earne gelicost
        on geoguðe nu   gleaw geworden.

118:175 Leofað sawul min   and ðe lustum hereð,
        and me þine domas   dædum fultumiað.

118:176 Ic gedwelede   swa þæt dysige sceap,
        þæt ðe forwurðan   wolde huru;
        la, sec þinne esne   elne, drihten,
        forðon ic ðinra beboda ne forgeat   beorhtra æfre.

121:7   Sy ðe on ðinum mægne sib   mæst and fyrmest
        and on þinum torrum wese   tidum genihtsum.

Psalm from Vp, (Krapp, p.128)

133:1   Efne bletsien nu   bliðe drihten
        ealle his agene   onbyhtscealcas.

133:2   Ge þe on godes huse   gearwe standað,
        and on cafertunum   Cristes huses
        ures þæs halgan godes   held begangað.

133:3   Hebbað neodlice   nihta gehwylcere
        eowre handa   on halig lof
        and bletsiað   balde drihten.

133:4   Ge bletsige   bliðe drihten
        of Sionbeorge   symble æt þearfe,
        se þe heofon worhte,   hrusan swylce.

Psalm-fragments from Vj (Dobbie, p.86)

139:1   Genere me wið niþe   on naman þinum,
        fram yfelum men,   ece drihten.

140:2   Sy on ðinre gesihðe   mines sylfes gebed
        full ricene gereht,   swa recels bið,
        þonne hit gifre   gleda bærnað.

Psalms from Vp (Krapp, pp.148-150)

148:1 Heriað ge on heofenum   hælend drihten,
       heriað hlude   on heanessum.

148:2 Heriað hine ealle   engla ðreatas,
       lofige hine swylce   eall his leodmægen.

148:3 Herigen hine swylce   sunna and mona,
       æghwylc steorra   and þæt æðele leoht.

148:4 Heofenas hine heofena   herian georne,
       and þa wæter swylce   ðe ofer wolcnum synt
       of heofenhame,   herigen drihten.

148:5 Forðon he sylfa cwæð,   sona wærun
       wræclice geworht   wætera ðryþe,
       and gesceapene wærun,   þa he sylfa het.

148:6 Þa he on ecnesse   eall staðelade
       and on worulda woruld   wolde healdan;
       he sette bebod,   syþþan heo þæt heoldon.

148:7 Herigen dracan swylce   drihten of eorðan,
       and ealle neowelnessa   herian naman drihtnes.

148:8 Fyr, forst, hægel   and gefeallen snaw,
       is and yste,   ealra gastas
       þe his word willað   wyrcean georne.

148:9 Muntas and geswyru,   micle beamas,
       þa þe mæst and wæstm   mannum bringað,
       and on eallum cedrum   ciið alædeð.

148:10 Deor and neat,   do þæt sniome;
       nifle nædran cynn   be naman ealle,
       and fugla cynn   fiðerum gescyrped.

148:11 Eorðcyningas eac   ealle swylce
       þe folcum her   fore wisien
       and ealdormen   ahwær syndan,
       and ealle þe þas eorþan   ahwær demeð.

148:12 Beon ge, hægestealdas   and glade fæmnan,
       ealde and geonge   ealle ætsamne;
       herian naman drihtnes   mid neodlofe.

148:13   Forþon his anes nama   ofer ealle is
         ahafen healice   hæleða ealra:
         is upp ahafen   his andetness
         heah ofer myclum   heofone and eorðan.

148:14   He horn hefeð   holdes folces,
         he lofe leohteð   leofe þa halgan;
         wese awa frið   on Israhela
         fælum folce,   and hi forð heonan
         on his neaweste   neode wunian.

149:1   Singað samheorte   sangas drihtne
         and him neowne sang   nu ða singað;
         wese his herenes   on haligra
         clænre cyricean   cyðed geneahhe.

149:2   Israhelas on hine   eac blissien,
         and Sione bearn   symble hihtan
         swiðust ealra.

149:3   Herigen his naman   neode on ðreatum,
         on timpano   tidum heriað
         and on psalterio   singað georne.

149:4   Forðon on his folc is   fægere drihtne
         wel licendlic,   and he wynlice
         þam manþwærum syleð   mære hælu.

149:5   Ðonne on wuldre gefeoð   wel þa halgan,
         beoð on heora husum   bliðe gedreme.

149:6   Hi on gomum bið   godes oft bemynd;
         heo þæs wislice   wynnum brucað,
         and sweord habbaþ   swylce on folmum.

149:7   Mid þy hi wrecan þenceað   wraðum cynnum
         and ðrea þearle   þeodum eawan.

149:8   And hio bindan   balde þenceað
         cyningas on campum,   and cuðlice,
         heora æðelingas don   on isene bendas.

149:9   Þæt hio dom on him   deopne gecyðan
         and þæt mid wuldre   awriten stande:
         þis is haligra wuldor   her on eorðan.

150:1   Heriað on þam halgum   his holdne drihten,
         heriað hine on his mægenes   mære hælu.

150:2   Heriað hine swylce   on his heahmihtum,
         heriað hine æfter mode   his mægenþrymmes.

150:3   Heriað hine on hleoðre   holdre beman
         ....(LACUNA)

Bibliography

EDITIONS

Assmann, Bruno, ed. Die Handschrift von Exeter, Metra des Boetius, Salamo und Saturn, Die Psalmen. Bibliotek der angelsächsischen Poesie, herausgeben von Richard Paul Wülker. 3 Band. Leipzig: 1898.

Bateson, Mary, ed. Ælfric's Letter to the Monks of Eynsham in Kitchin, ed., Obedientary Rolls of St. Swithun's. Hampshire Record Society: 1892.

Birch, W. de G., ed. The Liber Vitae of Hyde Abbey, Winchester. Hampshire Record Society: 1892.

Breck, E., ed. Translation of Æthelwold's De consuetudine monachorum. Leipzig: 1887.

Brenner, E., ed. Die altenglische Junius-Psalter. Anglistische Forschungen 23: Heidelberg: 1908.

Bright, James and Robert L. Ramsay, eds. Liber Psalmorum: The West Saxon Psalms. Boston: 1900.

Brock, E., ed. The Blickling Psalter in R. Morris, ed. The Blickling Homilies. Early English Text Society original series 58, 63, 73. London: 1874-1880.

Campbell, A. P., ed. The Tiberius Psalter. Ottawa: 1974.

Caro, G., ed. "Die Varianten der Durhamer HS und des Tiberiusfragments der ae. Prosaversion der Benedictinerregel." Englische Studien 24 (1898), pp.161-176.

Cockayne, O., ed. Leechdoms, Wortcunning and Starcraft of Early England. Rolls Series 35: 1864-1866.

Colgrave, Bertram et al., eds. The Paris Psalter. Early English Manuscript Facsimile series 8. Copenhagen: 1958.

Dobbie, E., ed. The Anglo-Saxon Minor Poems. Anglo-Saxon Poetic Records VI. New York: 1942.

Feiler, E., ed. Das Benediktiner-Offizium, eine altenglisches Brevier aus dem 11 Jahrhundert. Anglistische Forschungen 4. Heidelberg: 1901.

Grein, Christian W. M., ed. Bibliotek der angelsächsischen Poesie. 2 Band. Göttingen: 1858.

Harsley, F., ed. Eadwine's Canterbury Psalter. E.E.T.S. o.s. 92. London: 1889.

James, M. R., ed. The Canterbury Psalter. Oxford: 1935.

Kimmens, A. C., ed. An edition of the British Museum MS Stowe 2: The Stowe Psalter. Dissertation Abstracts 30 (1969), 1139A (Princeton dissertation).

Krapp, G. P., ed. The Paris Psalter and the Meters of Boethius. A.S.P.R. V. New York: 1932.

Kuhn, Sherman M., ed. The Vespasian Psalter. Ann Arbor, Michigan: 1965.

Liles, Bruce, ed. The Canterbury Psalter: an edition with notes and glossary. DA 28 (1967), 1053A (Stanford diss.)

Lindelöf, U., ed. Die altenglischen Glossen im Bosworth-Psalter. Mémoires de la Société Néophilologique de Helsingfors 5 (1909), pp.137-230.

Lindelöf, U., ed. Der Lambeth-Psalter. Acta Societatis Scientiarum Fennicae 35.i and 43.iii. Helsinki: 1909-1914.

Logeman, W. S., ed. De Consuetudine Monachorum. Anglia 13 (1891), pp.365-454, and Anglia 15 (1893), pp.20-40.

Napier, A. S., ed. The Old English Version, with the Latin Original, of the Enlarged Rule of Chrodegang etc. E.E.T.S. o.s. 150. London: 1916.

Oess, G., ed. Die altenglische Arundel-Psalter. Anglistische Forschungen 30. Heidelberg: 1910.

Plummer, C., ed. Two of the Saxon Chronicles Parallel. Oxford: 1892-1899. Reprinted D. Whitelock, ed. Oxford: 1952.

Raine, J., ed. Historians of the Church of York. Rolls Series 71. London: 1879, volume 1.

Roeder, F., ed. Die altenglische Regius-Psalter. Studien zur englischen Philologie 18. Halle: 1904.

Rosier, J. L., ed. The Vitellius Psalter. Cornell Studies in English 42. Ithaca: 1962.

Schröer, A., ed. "De Consuetudine Monachorum". Englische Studien 9 (1886), pp.294-296.

Schröer, A., ed. Die angelsächsischen Prosarbeitungen der Benediktinerregel. Bibl. der ags. Prosa 2. Kassel: 1885-1888. Repr. H. Gneuss, ed. Darmstadt: 1964.

Schröer, A., ed. Die Wintney-Version der Regula Sancti Benedicti. Halle: 1888.

Sisam, Kenneth and Celia, eds. The Salisbury Psalter. E.E.T.S. 242. Oxford: 1959.

Spelman, J., ed. Psalterium Davidis Latino-saxonicum vetus. 1640.

Stubbs, W., ed. Memorials of St. Dunstan. Rolls Series 63. London: 1874.

Sweet, Henry, ed. The Oldest English Texts. E.E.T.S. o.s. 83. London: 1885.

Symons, Dom Thomas, ed. The Monastic Agreement of the Monks and Nuns of the English Nation. London: 1953.

Thorpe, Benjamin, ed. Libri Psalmorum versio antiqua Latina: cum Paraphrasi Anglo-Saxonica, partim soluta oratione, partim metrice composita. Oxford: 1835.

Ure, James, ed. The Benedictine Office: an Old English Text. Edinburgh University Publications in Language and Literature 11. Edinburgh: 1957.

Wildhagen, K., ed. Der Cambridger-Psalter. Bibl. der. ags. Prosa 7. Hamburg: 1910.

Winterbottom, Michael, ed. Three Lives of English Saints. Toronto: 1972.

Wright, David et al., eds. The Vespasian Psalter. E.E.M.F. 14. Copenhagen: 1967

Zupitza, J., ed. "Ein weiteres Bruchstück der Regularis Concordia in altenglische Sprache". Archiv. 84 (1890), pp.2-16.

CRITICAL AND LINGUISTIC COMMENTARY

Bartlett, H. The Metical Division of the Paris Psalter. Baltimore: 1896.

Bateson, Mary. "Rules for Monks and Secular Canons after the Revival under King Edgar". English Historical Review 9 (1894), pp.690-708.

Bruce, J. D. "Immediate and Ultimate Source of the Rubrics and Introductions to the Psalms of the Paris Psalter". Modern Language Notes 8 (1893), pp.72-82.

Bruce, J. D. "The Anglo-Saxon Version of the Book of Psalms, commonly known as the Paris Psalter". Publications of the Modern Language Association 9 (1894), pp.43-164.

Bullough, D. A. "The Educational Tradition in England from Alfred to Ælfric: Teaching Utrisque Linguæ". Settimane di Studio del Centro Italiano di Studi sull'Alto Medioevo 19 (1972), pp.466-478.

Collins, R. L: "A Reexamination of the Old English Glosses in the Blickling Psalter". Anglia 81, (1963), pp.124-128.

Diamond, Robert. The Poetic Diction of the Anglo-Saxon Metrical Psalms. The Hague: 1963.

Dietrich, F. "Hycgan und Hopian". Zeitschrift für deutsches Altertum 9 (1852), pp.214-222.

Fehr, B. Die Hirtenbriefe Aelfrics in altenglischer und lateinischer Fassung. Bibl. der ags. Prosa 9. Hamburg: 1914.

Förster, Max. "Die altenglischen Texte der Pariser National-Bibliotek". Englische Studien 62 (1927), pp.113-131.

Gneuss, Helmut. Lehnbildungen und Lehnbedeutungen in altenglischen. Berlin: 1955.

Gneuss, Helmut. "The Origin of Standard Old English and Æthelwold's School at Winchester". Anglo-Saxon England 1 (1972), pp.63-83.

Gretsch, Mechthild. "Æthelwold's Translation of the Regula Sancti Benedicti and its Latin Exemplar". Anglo-Saxon England 3 (1974), pp.125-151.

Gretsch, Mechthild. Die Regula Sancti Benedicti in England und ihre altenglische Übersetzung. Munich: 1973.

Jordan, Richard. Eigentümlichkeiten des anglischen Wortschatzes. Anglistische Forschungen 17: 1906. Reprinted Amsterdam: 1967.

Keim, H. W. "Æthelwold und die Mönchreform in England". Anglia 41 (1921), pp.405-443.

Korhammer, Michael. "The Origin of the Bosworth Psalter". Anglo-Saxon England 2 (1973), pp.173-187.

Liebermann, F. "Æthelwolds Anhang zur Benedictinerregel". Archiv 108 (1904), pp.375-377.

Lindelöf, U. Studien zu altenglischen Psalterglossen. Bonner Beiträge zur Anglistik 13. Bonn: 1904.

Parsons, David, ed. Tenth-Century Studies: Essays in Commemoration of the Council of Winchester and the Regularis Concordia. Chichester: 1975.

Ramsay, Robert L. "The Latin Text of the Paris Psalter: A Collation and some Conclusions". American Journal of Philology 41 (1920), pp.147-176.

Schabram, Hans. Die dialektale und zeitliche Verbreitung des Worguts. Superbia 1. Munich: 1965.

Schabram, Hans. "Etymologie und Kontextanalyse in der altenglischen Semantik". Zeitschrift für vergleichende Sprachforschung 84 (1970), pp.233-253.

Schröer, A. "Die angelsächsischen Prosarbeitungen der Benedictinerregel". Englische Studien 14 (1891), pp.241-253.

Sievers, E. Die angelsächsischen Benediktinerregel. Tübingen: 1887.

Sievers, E. "Zur Rhythmik des germanischen Alliterationsverses". Beiträge 10 (1885), pp.451-545.

Sisam, Kenneth. Studies in the History of Old English Literature. Oxford: 1953.

Symons, Dom Thomas. "Sources of the Regularis Concordia". Downside Review 59 (1941).

Tanger, Gustav. "Collation des Pariser altenglischen Psalters mit Thorpe's Ausgabe". Anglia 6 (1884), pp.125-141.

Tinkler, John D. Vocabulary and Syntax of the Old English Version in the Paris Psalter. Janua Linguarum series practica 67. The Hague: 1971.

Thomson, E. Godcunde Lar 7 Þeowdom: Select Monuments of the Doctrine and Worship of the Catholic Church in England before the Norman Conquest. London: 1849.

Tschischiwitz, Benno. Die Metrik der angelsächsischen Psalmenübersetzung. Breslau: 1908.

Tupper, F. "History and Texts of the Benedictine Reform in the Tenth Century". Modern Language Notes 8 (1893), pp.344-367.

Wildhagen, K. "Das Psalterium Gallicanum in England". Englische Studien 54 (1920), p.35 ff.

Wildhagen, K. Der Psalter des Eadwine von Canterbury. Halle: 1905.

Wildhagen K. Studien zum Psalterium Romanum in England und zu seinen Glossierungen, in Festschrift für Lorenz Morsbach. Studien zur englischen Philologie 50. Halle: 1913.

Zeuner, R. Die Sprache des kentischen Psalters. Halle: 1881.

HISTORICAL COMMENTARY

Batiffol, Pierre. History of the Roman Breviary. Transl. A.M.Y. Becylay. London: 1898.

Baümer, Dom S. Histoire du Bréviare. Transl. Dom R. Biron. Paris: 1905.

Blair, Peter Hunter. An Introduction to Anglo-Saxon England. Cambridge: 1962.

Deanesly, Margaret. Sidelights on the Anglo-Saxon Church. London: 1962.

Deanesly, Margaret. The PreConquest Church in England. London: 1961.

Godfrey, John. The Church in Anglo-Saxon England. Cambridge: 1962.

Knowles, Dom David. The Monastic Order in England. Cambridge. 1966.

Robinson, J. Armitage. The Times of St. Dunstan. Oxford: 1923.

Stenton, Sir Frank. Anglo-Saxon England. 3rd edition. Oxford: 1971.

SOURCE BOOKS

Anderson, George K. The Literature of the Anglo-Saxons. Princeton: 1966. First published 1949.

Cook, A. S. Biblical Quotations in Old English Prose Writers. London: 1898.

Cross, F. N., ed. The Oxford Dictionary of the Christian Church. London: 1958.

Garmonsway, G. N., trans. The Anglo-Saxon Chronicle. London: 1953.

Ker, N. R. A Catalogue of Manuscripts Containing Anglo-Saxon. Oxford: 1957.

Morrell, Minnie C. A Manual of Old English Biblical Materials. Knoxville: 1965.

Whitelock, Dorothy, ed. Sweet's Anglo-Saxon Reader in Prose and Verse. Oxford: 1967.